Are We There Yet?

Family Road-Trip Guide to America's Roadside
Oddities: Mystery Spots, Gravity Hills, UFO
Festivals & Abandoned Parks

Les Brady

Medialusion Group

Contents

Disclaimer

This book is intended for entertainment purposes only. While many of the places mentioned are real and can be visited, some locations, events, pictures, and stories have been dramatized, exaggerated, or fictionalized for storytelling and humor. Readers should verify the existence and details of attractions before visiting and exercise common sense when exploring offbeat destinations. The author and publisher are not responsible for any outcomes resulting from following the suggestions or stories in this book.

Now, back to the adventure!

Introduction: The Call of the Unusual

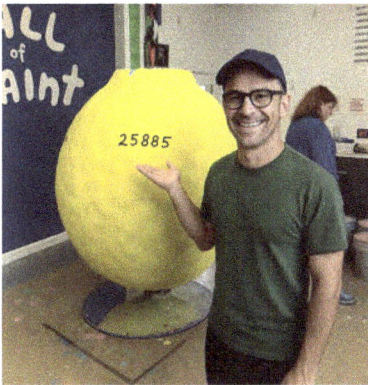

Let me tell you about the day I realized I had a problem with tourist traps. Back in 2017, I was standing in front of the World's Largest Ball of Paint in Alexandria[1], Indiana, contemplating how I'd managed to drive four hours out of my way to see what was essentially 20 years of accumulated house paint. The ball weighed over 5,000 pounds, housed in its own climate-controlled building, and I found myself completely mesmerized. That's when it hit me - I wasn't just casually interested in America's weirdest attractions; I was obsessed with them.

This wasn't just a one-time thing. My GPS history read like a who's who of roadside peculiarities: the World's Largest Pistachio in Alamogordo, New Mexico[2]; the mysterious Oregon Vortex[3] where water allegedly flows uphill; a museum in McLean, Texas dedicated entirely to barbed wire[4] (surprisingly more interesting than it sounds). My camera roll was filled with photos of me posing next to giant fiberglass animals, and my glove compartment overflowed with brochures from attractions that probably haven't updated their marketing materials since 1973.

But here's the thing: these 'tourist traps' that we're all supposed to be too sophisticated to enjoy are actually portals into the heart of American culture. Every oversized lawn ornament and mysterious gravity-defying shack conceal a story about dreamers, schemers, and communities united by the wonderfully weird. These places aren't just stops along the highway; they're chapters in an ongoing story about who we are as a nation of unabashed oddball enthusiasts.

This book is your guide to embracing the strange, the oversized, and the inexplicably fascinating corners of America. We'll explore everything from abandoned theme parks to museums dedicated to the most unlikely collections. You'll learn how to spot the difference between a genuinely charming tourist trap and a cynical money grab, discover the best times to visit (hint: the off-season often reveals the true character of these places), and maybe even gain a deeper appreciation for why humans feel compelled to build giant balls of twine in the first place.

Along the way, I'll share the lessons learned from my own misadventures - like why you should always carry cash when visiting remote attractions (card readers and cellular signals don't always reach the World's Largest Whatever) and how sometimes the best stories come from getting spectacularly lost while trying to find these places. Consider this book your permission slip to exit the highway, ignore your GPS's plaintive requests to 'return to the route,' and discover the America that exists beyond the gift shop.

Prepare to embrace the strange, grab your camera, and fasten your seatbelt. Just keep in mind that the stories you will tell about the time you made the three-hour drive to see a gigantic concrete prairie dog are more important than the final destination. And those are usually the best stories, I promise you.

Chapter 1

Giants Among Us

America's Obsession with Oversized Roadside Art

S TANDING IN THE SHADOW of the **world's largest ball of twine** in Cawker City, Kansas[1], I couldn't help but wonder what cosmic force compels humans to create monumentally oversized versions of everyday objects. Perhaps it's the same impulse that drove ancient civilizations to build pyramids, except we Americans prefer our monuments in the shape of giant butter churns and concrete dinosaurs. As someone who's logged thousands of miles chasing these monumental oddities, I've discovered they're more than just marketing gimmicks or relics of mid-century roadside Americana. Each oversized attraction tells a distinctly American story of entrepreneurial spirit, small-town pride, and the eternal quest to stand out in a country that values the superlative above all else.

Take the **Enchanted Highway** in Regent, North Dakota[2], where retired schoolteacher Gary Greff has spent decades creating massive metal sculptures that stretch for 32 miles across the prairie. These towering structures, including 'Geese in Flight' and 'Fisherman's Dream,' weren't just artistic expressions – they were a calculated attempt to save his dying hometown of Regent by giving travelers a reason to exit the interstate. The strategy worked: tourism increased, a small gift shop opened, and suddenly a town of 150 people had something besides grain elevators to put on their postcards.

The phenomenon of roadside giants traces back to the golden age of automobile travel, when highways like Route 66 transformed how Americans experienced their country. Local businesses, desperate to catch the eye of passing motorists, realized that bigger meant better when it came to roadside architecture. Paul Bunyan statues wielded massive axes outside logging museums, while colossal coffee pots steamed atop rural diners. These weren't just attractions; they were survival strategies for small towns watching their lifeblood redirect to new interstate systems.

In our GPS-guided, review-driven travel culture, these analog attractions might seem like relics. But there's something refreshingly honest about a 40-foot-tall bowling pin that exists solely to make you pull over and investigate. Unlike modern tourist traps engineered by marketing teams, these roadside giants sprang from genuine local pride and entrepreneurial desperation – a combination that often yields the most fascinating results.

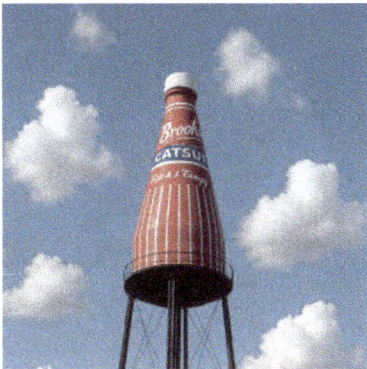

My misadventures photographing these monuments have taught me that the real treasures aren't always the attractions themselves, but the stories behind them. In Collinsville, Illinois, home to the world's **largest ketchup bottle**[3], I met an entire preservation society dedicated to protecting their 170-foot-tall condiment from demolition. These weren't just preservationists; they were story keepers, protecting a piece of their community's identity with the same fervor others might reserve for historical mansions or battlefield sites.

Navigating to these attractions often feels like a scavenger hunt designed by a particularly mischievous road trip deity. Paper maps become essential backups when GPS fails, and asking for directions at local gas stations turns into an adventure in itself. I've learned to trust hand-drawn maps on diner napkins more than my smartphone's confident but often misguided assertions about where exactly one might find a three-story-tall rocking chair.

So grab your camera, pack some snacks, and prepare for a journey through a landscape where size definitely matters. We're about to explore the stories behind America's most audacious roadside attractions – monuments to creativity, commerce, and the undying human desire to build things that make people stop their cars and say, 'Would you look at that?'

The Golden Age of Roadside Giants: How Highway Culture Birthed Massive Attractions

I first stumbled across **Lucy the Elephant**[4] while trying to find a bathroom in Margate, New Jersey. There she stood in all her glory: six stories of architectural audacity, complete with windows for eyes and a howdah that doubled as an observation deck. Built in 1881 by real estate developer James Lafferty, this magnificent pachyderm wasn't just America's first roadside giant – she was a testament to the kind of creative marketing that would define American highway culture for the next century .Americans have always had a thing for the colossal, but it took the **Federal Aid Road Act of 1916**[5] to turn that obsession into a legitimate business strategy. Suddenly, the country had 150,000 miles of fresh pavement to explore, and enterprising business owners realized they needed more than just a 'Gas, Food, Lodging' sign to lure travelers off these new highways.

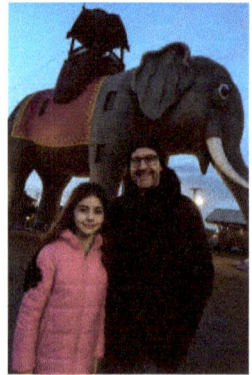

The post-World War II economic boom launched us into the golden age of roadside colossi. Veterans returned home with disposable income and a desire to see their country, while the newly minted middle class had both cars and paid vacation time. The stage was set for an arms race of architectural absurdity. Want to sell hot dogs? Better build your stand in the shape of a giant wiener. Running a motel? Why not construct it as a concrete teepee village?

These weren't just random acts of architectural eccentricity – they were calculated survival strategies. When I interviewed the grandson of the man who built the **World's Largest Prairie Dog**[6] in Oakley, Kansas, in 2009, he revealed that their gift shop's earnings tripled the day they installed the 40-foot-tall concrete rodent. 'People would drive past ten other identical souvenir stands,' he told me, 'but they couldn't resist stopping at ours. Something about that giant prairie dog just demanded attention.'

The Interstate Highway System's arrival in the 1960s threatened to bypass these beloved attractions into obsolescence. Many didn't survive the rerouting of America's travel patterns. Yet, something remarkable happened: instead of disappearing entirely, these roadside giants became symbols of local pride and identity. Communities rallied to preserve their oversized landmarks, recognizing that these quirky colossi were more than just tourist traps – they were part of America's cultural DNA.

Today, while new roadside giants still occasionally appear (I recently visited a **40-foot-tall baseball bat in Louisville** that was built in the 1990s), the real joy comes from seeking out the surviving monuments of the golden age. Some, like the Brooks Catsup Bottle Water Tower in Collinsville, Illinois, have earned spots on the National Register of Historic Places. Others survive through the dedication of local preservation societies who understand that these attractions, however kitschy, tell important stories about American ingenuity and entrepreneurship.Documenting these roadside behemoths has taught me that timing and patience are essential. Many are maintained by small towns or individual owners operating on limited budgets, so calling ahead isn't just courteous – it's necessary. I once drove three hours to photograph a **giant coffee pot in Bedford, Pennsylvania**[7], only to find it temporarily dismantled for repairs. The silver lining? The local diner owner who spotted me staring dejectedly at the empty platform shared stories about the pot's history over a consolation slice of pie.

For today's road-trippers, these attractions offer something increasingly rare in our digitally mediated world: genuine surprise and delight. In an era where most tourist experiences are thoroughly documented on social media before we ever arrive, there's something magical about rounding a bend and coming face-to-knee with a concrete giant you never knew existed. These roadside colossi remind us that sometimes the best travel experiences aren't found at our carefully planned destinations, but in the wonderfully weird discoveries we make along the way.

Marketing in Mammoth Proportions: The Business Strategy Behind Oversized Art

Let me tell you about the day I discovered the true genius behind America's obsession with mammoth marketing. I was interviewing the owner of a small-town hardware store that had installed a 20-foot wrench on their roof back in 1952. 'That wrench paid for my kids' college education,' he told me, completely straight-faced. 'Cost us $3,000 to build. Made it back in additional sales within three months.'

The psychology behind oversized attractions is deceptively simple: in a world of endless distractions, nothing demands attention quite like something absurdly large. It's the architectural equivalent of someone shouting in a library – your brain can't help but notice. Long before viral marketing was a buzzword, these roadside giants were generating word-of-mouth advertising that modern social media managers would kill for.

Take the infamous **Longaberger Basket Building in Newark, Ohio**[8]. When the Longaberger Company decided to build their headquarters in the shape of a giant basket – complete with handles – it seemed like corporate whimsy gone wild. But that seven-story basket became their most powerful marketing tool, earning millions in free publicity and turning their office into a tourist destination. Though the company later faced challenges, that basket remains an icon of architectural advertising audacity.

The strategy wasn't limited to corporate giants. Small businesses discovered that going big could level the playing field. In Minnesota, I met a dairy farmer who installed a 40-foot fiberglass cow on his property in 1965. 'Changed everything,' he explained. 'Suddenly we weren't just another dairy – we were the dairy with the giant cow. People would drive from three counties over just to buy milk under that cow.'

During the pre-internet era, these colossal creations served as analog hashtags, making businesses not just memorable but photographable. Travelers would snap pictures, show them to friends back home, and inadvertently become unpaid marketing ambassadors. One motel owner told me his 30-foot neon cactus generated more business through vacation slideshows than all his newspaper ads combined.

But here's what fascinates me most: these oversized advertisements often outlived their original purpose to become beloved landmarks. **The Big Duck of Long Island**[9], built in 1931 to sell poultry products, hasn't housed a duck farm in decades. Yet it remains a fiercely protected piece of local heritage, proof that sometimes the marketing becomes more valuable than the product it was meant to sell.

Modern businesses still occasionally embrace this bigger-is-better philosophy, though with contemporary twists. When I visited the **World's Largest Hockey Stick in Eveleth, Minnesota**[10], I found it had been deliberately designed to be social media-friendly, with perfect photo angles and hashtag suggestions painted right on the viewing area. The old strategy adapts to new technologies, but the core insight remains: size gets attention.

For travelers seeking these monuments to marketing ingenuity, I've learned a few vital tips.

1. First, always check if the attraction is still standing – these giants occasionally succumb to weather or development.

2. Second, visit during off-peak hours for the best photos; early morning light tends to be particularly flattering to forty-foot-tall ice cream cones.

3. Finally, take time to chat with locals – they often have fascinating stories about how these massive marketing tools shaped their communities.

The brilliance of oversized advertising lies in its straightforward audacity. In an age of targeted ads and algorithm-driven marketing, there's something refreshingly honest about a giant hammer on your roof announcing 'We sell hardware here.' These marketing mammoths remind us that sometimes the boldest strategy is also the simplest: make it big enough, and they'll come.

Planning Your Colossal Road Trip: Maps, Routes, and Tips for Giant-Hunting

After three decades of chasing oversized attractions across America, I've learned that hunting giants requires equal parts preparation and spontaneity. You might think finding a 55-foot-tall coffee pot would be straightforward – after all, how many giant percolators can one country contain? (The answer, surprisingly, is more than you'd expect.)

Picture this: you're cruising down a dusty highway, armed with nothing but determination and a vague notion that somewhere nearby stands the World's Largest Ball of Twine. Your GPS confidently declares 'You have arrived' while pointing to an empty cornfield. Welcome to the peculiar world of giant-hunting, where technology and reality often have competing interpretations of geography.

The **RoadsideAmerica.com** database has become an indispensable tool for serious giant-hunters, offering coordinates and visitor tips for thousands of oversized attractions.

But here's a pro tip:

Always cross-reference with local tourism websites. That 30-foot-tall hammer might have been relocated to make room for a 40-foot-tall wrench, and sometimes only the locals keep track of these colossal musical chairs.

I've found that planning a giant-hunting expedition works best when you think in clusters. The Midwest, particularly along the old Route 66 corridor, offers the densest concentration of roadside colossi. You can string together visits to enormous boots, colossal ketchup bottles, and mammoth mailboxes like an architectural scavenger hunt. My personal record is eight giants in one day – though I wouldn't recommend such an ambitious pace unless you have a particular fondness for gas station coffee and hurried photography.

Keep a physical atlas in your car. Yes, really. When you're searching for the **World's Largest Holstein Cow in New Salem, North Dakota**[11] and your phone loses signal, that paper map becomes your best friend. I once navigated to the **World's Largest Buffalo in Jamestown**[12] using nothing but an old Rand McNally and directions from a particularly enthusiastic convenience store clerk who drew me a map on my coffee receipt.

Documentation is crucial – not just for your own memories but for future giant-hunters. I maintain a travel journal noting important details like parking locations, best photography angles, and whether that '24/7' access actually means 'whenever Earl feels like unlocking the gate.' Some attractions require special timing: the World's Largest Pistachio in New Mexico casts its most dramatic shadow at sunset, while Minnesota's Paul Bunyan is best photographed in early morning light before tour buses arrive.

Weather can dramatically impact your giant-hunting success rate. That **65-foot-tall muskie in Hayward, Wisconsin**[13], looks considerably less impressive in a downpour, and snow can transform a simple photo stop into an impromptu arctic expedition. I learned this lesson the hard way after driving four hours through a blizzard to visit the **World's Largest Six-Pack**[14], in La Crosse, Wisconsin, only to find it wrapped in winter protection tarps.

Don't skip the visitor centers and local diners near these attractions. They're goldmines of information about other nearby giants that might not appear in your research. Plus, the stories you'll hear from locals about their beloved behemoths often become more memorable than the attractions themselves. I once spent two hours in a Kansas diner listening to the tale of how their giant grasshopper survived a tornado – the grasshopper photo took five minutes, but that story has lasted years.

Most importantly, embrace the unexpected detours. Some of my favorite discoveries have come from spotting hand-painted signs pointing to 'BIG THING THIS WAY' or following up on gas station attendants' enthusiastic recommendations. That's how I found myself face-to-face with a 20-foot-tall bowling pin in rural Missouri that wasn't listed in any guidebook.

Always carry cash for admission fees or donation boxes – many of these attractions are maintained by small towns or passionate individuals operating on shoestring budgets. And remember, these oversized oddities are often points of genuine pride for their communities.

Show respect for the locals who maintain these roadside wonders, no matter how quirky they might seem.

And if you're planning an extended giant-hunting expedition, consider investing in a wide-angle lens. Trust me on this one – you haven't known true frustration until you've tried to fit a 55-foot-tall penguin into a standard camera frame while backed against a fence. Though sometimes these photographic challenges lead to creative solutions – I've gotten some of my best shots while lying flat on my back in parking lots, much to the amusement of passing tourists.

Pulling into my driveway after another marathon giant-hunting expedition, I found myself reflecting on what drives us to create and preserve these mammoth monuments to American ingenuity. Maybe it's our inherent desire to leave a mark on the landscape, to say 'we were here' in the boldest way possible. Or perhaps it's something simpler – the pure joy of building something that makes strangers stop their cars and smile.

I've learned that these roadside giants are more than just supersized novelties; they're anchors of community identity and living testaments to American entrepreneurship. From the determined shopkeeper who bet his savings on a rooftop wrench to the retired schoolteacher crafting metal sculptures along a lonely highway, each creator saw possibility where others saw empty space. Their oversized dreams didn't just attract tourists – they created landmarks that transformed towns from dots on a map into destinations.

The continued preservation of these colossal curiosities speaks to something essential in our national character. In an era of cookie-cutter tourist experiences and algorithm-recommended attractions, these handcrafted giants remind us that creativity doesn't need corporate backing or focus group approval. Sometimes all it takes is a wild idea, some engineering moxie, and a community willing to embrace the extraordinary.

The next time you're planning a road trip, consider veering off the interstate to seek out these tremendous treasures. Pack your camera, bring plenty of snacks, and be prepared for GPS betrayal. You might not find every giant you're looking for, but I guarantee you'll discover something even more valuable: stories of American ingenuity, community pride, and the enduring power of thinking big – sometimes literally.

As for me, I've got my eye on a newly constructed 50-foot-tall garden gnome in Iowa. The locals say it's best photographed at sunrise, which means another pre-dawn departure in my future. But that's the thing about giant-hunting – once you start, the road ahead always seems to lead to something bigger and better.

Chapter 2

Mystery Spots and Gravity Hills

Where Physics Goes on Vacation

A S MY WATER BOTTLE MOVED UPHILL AND I STOOD AT A 45-DEGREE AN-GLE, I COULDN'T HELP BUT WONDER IF I HAD UNINTENTIONALLY WAN-DERED INTO A MATRIX GLITCH. THE MYSTERY SPOT in Santa Cruz, California[1] , is just one of many gravitational anomalies across America where tourists willingly pay good money to feel dizzy and question everything they know about physics. These mysterious spots scattered across America have been enchanting and confounding visitors for generations, each promoting its own unique brand of physics-defying phenomena. Whether attributed to magnetic anomalies, alien technology, or tears in the space-time continuum, these attractions masterfully blend scientific curiosity with old-fashioned showmanship.

I've encountered my fair share of these gravita-tional oddities, documenting each visit with an arsenal of measuring tools and a healthy dose of skepticism. What fascinates me most isn't just the clever illusions, but the way these places transform even the most hardened cynics into wide-eyed wonderers. Watch any group for more than a few minutes, and you'll witness the same pattern:

1. First comes the confident smirk

2. Then he furrowed brow of confusion

3. And finally, that moment of childlike delight when they decide to embrace the inexplicable.

Take the House of Mystery in Gold Hill, Oregon[2], where I witnessed a stoic physics professor completely lose his composure trying to explain why his water bottle kept rolling uphill.

Or the peculiar scene at Confusion Hill in California[3], where a group of engineers spent two hours arguing about angles while their kids simply enjoyed the topsy-turvy experience. At these spots, you'll find tourists performing an amusing ballet of stumbles and overcorrections as their brains try to reconcile what they're seeing with what they know should be possible.

For those planning to explore these gravitational anomalies, I've learned a few essential tricks.

1. First, eat light – nothing ruins the magic like motion sickness.

2. Second, wear comfortable shoes with good grip; you'll be doing plenty of leaning and stumbling.

3. And third, bring a camera with a level horizon indicator – it'll make for some mind-bending photos that'll confuse your social media followers for weeks.

In this chapter, we'll discuss America's most famous gravity-defying spots. I'll share insights on the best times to visit (hint: sunrise tours offer the most dramatic effects), how to capture those impossible-looking photos, and, most importantly, how to maintain your equilibrium while your sense of reality gets thoroughly scrambled. We'll go deep into the psychology behind these illusions, explore why our brains are so easily fooled, and

maybe even uncover a few secrets about how these mysterious spots work their magic –
though sometimes, as I've learned, it's more fun to let the mystery remain unsolved.

The Science Behind the Spots: Understanding Optical Illusions and Forced Perspective

Let me tell you about the day my brain went full pretzel trying to understand these gravity-defying tourist spots. Picture this: I'm standing in Oregon's House of Mystery, in Gold Hill, armed with a carpenter's level, three different compass apps, and enough scientific determination to make Neil deGrasse Tyson proud. My mission? To prove once and for all that it's all smoke, mirrors, and clever marketing.

Here's the reality behind these mind-bending attractions: they're masterclasses in perceptual manipulation. Your brain, that overconfident supercomputer between your ears, relies heavily on visual cues to make sense of the world. When these spots deliberately remove or distort your usual reference points - like true vertical lines and clear horizons - your mind starts making some questionable judgment calls.

The secret sauce is a combination of precisely engineered angles and carefully constructed environments. The buildings are typically built at specific tilts, usually between 15 and 25 degrees. When you step inside, your brain desperately tries to compensate for this slant by treating the tilted surfaces as level ground. The result? Everything else appears to defy gravity.

I watched a retired engineering professor completely lose his cool at the Oregon Vortex when his plumb bob refused to hang straight. 'This is preposterous!' he kept muttering, while his grandkids gleefully rolled marbles 'uphill.' The truth is, those marbles were actually rolling downhill - we were just standing in a tilted room that made downhill look like uphill. It's like trying to judge distances while wearing those funhouse mirror glasses, except instead of distorting your reflection, these places distort your entire sense of spatial awareness.

The real magic comes from forced perspective - a technique that's been messing with human perception since the ancient Egyptians were building pyramids. Think of those tourist photos where people appear to be holding up the Leaning Tower of Pisa. Same principle, just applied on a larger, more elaborate scale. These spots use strategically placed windows, artificially skewed horizon lines, and carefully angled walls to create environments where nothing quite adds up.

During one visit to the Santa Cruz Mystery Spot, in 2007, I watched a group of teenagers trying to take the perfect 'defying gravity' selfie. After fifteen minutes of increasingly creative poses, one of them accidentally discovered that changing the phone's angle made everyone look like they were falling sideways, leading to an impromptu photo session that looked like a scene from *"Inception*. Meanwhile, I quietly tested the floor with my level, confirming what research has consistently shown - these places are essentially full-scale optical illusions, using the same principles that make M.C. Escher prints mess with your head.

The most fascinating part? Even when you understand the science, these spots don't lose their ability to disorient you. Your intellectual knowledge that it's all an illusion doesn't override your brain's instinctive response to visual cues. It's like knowing how a magic trick works but still feeling amazed when you see it performed.

For the truly curious (or stubbornly skeptical), I've found that visiting during early morning hours offers the clearest view of how these illusions work. The low angle of sunrise can sometimes reveal the true tilt of structures, especially if you position yourself where you can see both the mystery spot and surrounding landscape in the same view. Just don't point this out during regular tours - nobody likes a mystery spoiler, and sometimes understanding the mechanics of wonder doesn't make it any less wonderful.

America's Most Popular Mystery Spots and Gravity Hills: Where to Find Them

Ready to have your perception of reality thoroughly messed with? Let me guide you through America's most perplexing gravitational oddities, where the laws of physics seem to take extended coffee breaks and your inner ear gets a workout worthy of an Olympic gymnast.

Let's start with the granddaddy of all mystery spots - The Mystery Spot in Santa Cruz, California. Operating since 1940, this 150-foot circular area nestled in the redwood forest has perfected the art of making people wobble like newborn deer trying to find their footing. During my latest visit, I watched a group of quantum physicists become increasingly flustered as their sophisticated measuring equipment produced readings that made about as much sense as a chocolate teapot. The demonstrations here are genuinely mind-bending - I still can't explain why my water bottle kept rolling uphill, though I'm pretty sure it had nothing to do with the tour guide's theory about alien gravitational manipulators.

Category	Details
Name	The Mystery Spot
Location	Santa Cruz, California, USA
Type of Attraction	Tilted House / Gravity-Defying Optical Illusions
Established	1940
Size	Approx. 1 acre
Main Features	Tilted house, slanted floors, uphill-rolling balls
Scientific Appeal	Forced perspective, optical illusions, spatial disorientation
Tour Style	Guided walking tours (~45 minutes)
Opening Hours	Daily, 10:00 AM – 5:00 PM
Best Time to Visit	Weekday mornings or off-season
Accessibility	Not wheelchair accessible; some steep/sloped paths
Tickets (as of 2025)	Adults: ~$10; Kids (3–12): ~$8
Additional Tips	Wear flat shoes, eat lightly before visiting, bring a level for fun photos
Website	www.mysteryspot.com
Fun Fact	Allegedly located in a gravitational anomaly zone

Confusion Hill

Up north in Piercy, California, Confusion Hill lives up to its name with such dedication that even your GPS might get dizzy. This spot features not only gravity-defying phenomena but also claims to be home to the elusive 'chipalope' - a supposed antelope-chipmunk hybrid that, coincidentally, only exists within their property boundaries. While I can't verify the existence of this mysterious creature, I can confirm that my sense of balance took a vacation the moment I stepped inside their tilted house.

Category	Details
Name	Confusion Hill
Location	Piercy, California, USA (along U.S. Route 101)
Type of Attraction	Gravity House, Optical Illusions, Logging History Exhibit
Established	1949
Size	Multi-attraction site on wooded hillside
Main Features	Tilted House, Gravity-Defying Walkway, Chipalope Sightings
Scientific Appeal	Gravity illusions, off-kilter architecture, perceptual anomalies
Tour Style	Self-guided + optional narrated tours
Opening Hours	Daily (usually 9:00 AM – 5:00 PM; hours may vary by season)
Best Time to Visit	Spring or Fall (lighter crowds and comfortable weather)
Accessibility	Some steep areas; partially accessible
Tickets (as of 2025)	Adults: ~$6–$8; Kids: ~$4–$5
Extra Attractions	Redwood Shoe House, Mountain Train Ride (seasonal)
Website	www.confusionhill.com
Fun Fact	Once featured on *Gravity Falls*; home to the mythical "Chipalope"

The Oregon Vortex

The Oregon Vortex in Gold Hill holds the distinction of being one of America's oldest documented mystery spots. Here, I witnessed perhaps the most entertaining spectacle of my mystery spot adventures - a couple's height apparently changing by several inches as they switched positions. The husband was so convinced his wife had suddenly grown taller that he demanded she try on his shoes to prove they weren't standing on hidden platforms.

Pro tip: visit during golden hour when the lighting makes the demonstrations even more dramatic.

Category	Details
Name	The Oregon Vortex & House of Mystery
Location	Gold Hill, Oregon, USA
Type of Attraction	Mystery Spot / Optical Illusion Site
Established	1930
Size	~0.25 acres (but the "vortex" is said to cover ~165 ft in diameter)
Main Features	Tilted House, Height Change Illusions, Gravity Anomalies
Scientific Appeal	Visual and spatial illusions, magnetic field myths, forced perspective
Tour Style	Guided walking tours only (~45 minutes)
Opening Hours	March–October, Daily, 10:00 AM – 5:00 PM
Best Time to Visit	Spring or early fall for fewer crowds and better light
Accessibility	Limited; uneven terrain and slopes
Tickets (as of 2025)	Adults: ~$15; Kids (6–12): ~$10; under 5: Free
Additional Features	Gift shop, picnic area, photo ops
Website	www.oregonvortex.com
Fun Fact	Said to be a site where "horses won't enter" and compasses go wild

Cosmos Mystery Area

For those venturing into the heartland, the Cosmos Mystery Area[4] in South Dakota's Black Hills offers a particularly intense experience. I discovered this the hard way when I tried to stand 'normally' while my body insisted on leaning at a 45-degree angle. The tour guide, noticing my struggle, quipped, 'Welcome to the only place where falling over is actually standing straight.' As an added bonus, they've got a geode mine where you can

hunt for crystals - because apparently defying gravity works up an appetite for rock collecting.

Category	Details
Name	Cosmos Mystery Area
Location	Rapid City, South Dakota, USA (Black Hills area)
Type of Attraction	Gravity House / Optical Illusion Zone
Established	1952
Size	Small forested hillside with tilted structures
Main Features	Gravity-defying cabin, tilted rooms, height change illusions
Scientific Appeal	Perception tricks, forced perspective, disorienting angles
Tour Style	Guided 30-minute walking tours
Opening Hours	Spring–Fall (typically May–October), 9:00 AM – 5:00 PM
Best Time to Visit	Weekday mornings for fewer crowds and cooler temps
Accessibility	Uneven surfaces, limited wheelchair access
Tickets (as of 2025)	Adults: ~$13; Kids (5–11): ~$6.50; Under 5: Free
Bonus Attractions	Geode mine, gift shop, gemstone panning
Website	www.cosmosmysteryarea.com
Fun Fact	You'll feel like you're leaning even when standing "straight"—bring Dramamine if sensitive!

Gravity Hill

Looking for something a bit more mobile? Gravity hills scattered across the country offer their own brand of physics-defying fun. Pennsylvania's Gravity Hill[5] near New Paris is particularly impressive - I watched in amazement as my turned-off car appeared to roll uphill. A local told me about winter sledders who regularly experience the surreal sensation of sliding 'up' the hill, though I'd recommend saving that experiment for someone braver than myself.

Category	Details
Name	Gravity Hill
Location	Near New Paris, Bedford County, Pennsylvania, USA
Type of Attraction	Gravity Hill / Optical Illusion / Natural Phenomenon
Established	Popularized in the late 20th century (exact origins unknown)
Size	~Hundred-foot stretch of rural road
Main Features	Cars appear to roll uphill when in neutral; water flows "uphill"
Scientific Appeal	Visual illusion due to terrain and lack of true horizon
Tour Style	Self-guided – drive or bike to the spot and test the illusion yourself
Opening Hours	24/7, outdoor roadside location
Best Time to Visit	Daylight hours (easier to line up the illusion); spring and fall are ideal
Accessibility	Fully accessible by car or bike
Tickets (as of 2025)	Free
Exact Location	Gravity Hill Road (off Route 96), near New Paris, PA
Website/Listing	No official website – listed on RoadsideAmerica and Google Maps
Fun Fact	Locals say it's haunted or magnetic—skeptics say it's just a genius slope!

The Mystery Hole

Speaking of regional oddities, The Mystery Hole in Fayetteville, West Virginia, deserves special mention for its uniquely Appalachian approach to gravitational anomalies. The owner's storytelling rivals the physical phenomena in entertainment value, weaving tales about underground magnetic forces while visitors attempt to maintain their balance in what feels like a funhouse designed by Einstein after a long night out.

Category	Details
Name	The Mystery Hole
Location	Fayetteville, West Virginia (near New River Gorge Bridge)
Type of Attraction	Optical Illusion Cabin / Gravity Anomaly / Roadside Oddity
Year Established	1973
Experience Type	Humorous guided tour through slanted rooms and visual tricks
Main Features	Tilted house, gravity-defying rooms, kitschy decor, giant gorilla statue
Tour Duration	~30 minutes, guided only
Opening Season	May to October
Hours of Operation	10:00 AM – 5:00 PM (Closed Tuesdays)
Admission (2025)	Adults: ~$7 · Kids: ~$5 · Under 5: Free
Accessibility	Not wheelchair accessible; tight, sloped spaces
Parking	Free on-site
Extra Perks	Retro gift shop, roadside photo ops, murals, oddball humor
Website	No official site — check Facebook or Google Maps for current info
Fun Fact	The roadside mascot is a *giant gorilla*, and the inside decor feels like a funhouse from another dimension.

For those planning their own mystery spot adventures, I've learned a few essential tips the hard way. First, wear flat, grippy shoes - trying to navigate these spots in heels is like attempting to ice skate on marbles. Early morning visits tend to offer the best photo opportunities and smaller crowds. Keep your phone charged for photos, but don't rely too heavily on your device's level app - it might just have an existential crisis. Most importantly, bring your sense of humor along with your sense of wonder. Whether you're a skeptic armed with scientific explanations or someone who prefers to believe in the mysterious, these destinations offer a uniquely American brand of roadside wonder.

Just remember, motion sickness medication should be taken before, not after, you start feeling dizzy. Trust me, watching water flow uphill on an empty stomach while your inner ear stages a revolt is an experience best avoided. Been there, done that, bought the tilted t-shirt.

Tips for Visiting: Best Times, Photo Opportunities, and Avoiding Motion Sickness

Let me share some hard-earned wisdom about visiting these gravitational wonderlands without turning your stomach into a physics experiment of its own. After countless visits (and a few regrettable lunch choices), I've developed a survival guide that'll help you make the most of your reality-bending adventure.

Best Times to Visit

Timing is everything when visiting these peculiar places. Early mornings offer two distinct advantages: cooler temperatures and dramatic lighting that enhances the visual illusions. There's something extra surreal about questioning physics before your morning coffee has kicked in. I once arrived at the Oregon Vortex right at opening time and had the entire place to myself - just me, the tour guide, and what felt like a tear in the space-time continuum.

Speaking of timing, avoid visiting during peak tourist season unless you enjoy watching strangers stumble around like newborn giraffes while waiting in long lines. Off-season weekday mornings are your best bet for both shorter wait times and optimal photo opportunities. Plus, smaller tour groups mean more time to experiment with different angles and positions without feeling rushed.

Photo Opportunities

Now, let's talk about capturing these mind-bending moments. Your phone's camera can work wonders, but here's a pro tip: **turn off your auto-horizon feature**. These spots are designed to mess with your perception, and your camera's helpful stabilization might actually work against you when trying to capture the full effect. I learned this the hard way after spending an hour trying to photograph a 'gravity-defying' ball roll, only to discover my phone had been helpfully 'correcting' the angle.

For the best shots:

- Position yourself where you can include both the anomalous effects and some normal reference points in the frame.

- Contrast makes the illusion more striking — think tilted houses against straight trees or water appearing to flow uphill against a level horizon.

- Bring a **wide-angle lens** if you've got one; these places often feel more cramped than your average tourist attraction, and you'll want to capture the full scope of the weirdness.

Avoiding Motion Sickness

Now for the elephant in the room: **motion sickness**. These places can turn even the most iron-stomached visitor into a wobbly mess. The visual-vestibular conflict created by these illusions is like trying to read *War and Peace* while riding a mechanical bull. Through extensive trial and error (mostly error), I've developed some strategies to keep your equilibrium somewhat intact:

- Take **motion sickness medication** before your visit — waiting until you're already dizzy is like closing the barn door after the horse has bolted and is currently throwing up in the parking lot.

- Eat a **light meal** beforehand; this isn't the time to test drive that new five-alarm chili restaurant you spotted on the drive in.

- During your visit, find **fixed reference points** outside the 'anomalous zones' when you start feeling wobbly. The horizon or distant trees work well — anything your brain can use to recalibrate its sense of what's level.

- Keep a supply of **ginger candies** in your travel bag; they're like little lifesavers for your stomach and won't mess with the experience like some stronger medications might.

- **Wear sensible footwear** — you'll be walking on tilted surfaces and trying to maintain your balance in ways your body isn't used to. Think 'mountain goat chic' rather than 'fashion forward.'

- **Take regular breaks** between demonstrations. Most spots have designated 'normal' areas where you can reset your spatial awareness. Use them.

- Bring **sunglasses** — trying to focus on optical illusions while squinting in bright sunlight is a recipe for extra dizziness.

Embrace the Experience

Remember, half the fun is letting yourself be amazed. Sure, you could spend your entire visit trying to debunk every illusion with your phone's level app (guilty as charged), but where's the fun in that? Sometimes the best travel experiences come from embracing the impossible, even when you know there's a perfectly logical explanation lurking behind the curtain.

Just keep in mind that while these attractions promise to defy the laws of physics, they still have to follow the **laws of operating hours**. Call ahead to check schedules, especially during off-season or inclement weather. There's nothing worse than driving hours to experience gravitational anomalies only to find that gravity is taking the day off.

Final Thoughts

As my visit to the Mystery Spot fades into memory, I find myself contemplating the peculiar allure of places where reality takes unexpected detours. These gravity-defying destinations offer more than just optical illusions and tilted rooms — they provide a refreshing reminder that sometimes the most memorable experiences come from surrendering our need to explain everything.

Through countless visits to these physics-defying attractions, I've discovered that the real magic lies not in the scientific explanations (though they're fascinating), but in the **shared experience of collective wonder**. There's something uniquely bonding about watching complete strangers transform from skeptics to wide-eyed adventurers, united in their delighted confusion as water rolls uphill and perspectives shift like desert mirages.

Whether you're a physics enthusiast armed with measuring tools or someone who simply enjoys the thrill of having your reality temporarily rearranged, America's mystery spots offer a uniquely entertaining escape from the ordinary. Pack your flat shoes, bring your motion sickness remedies, and prepare to question everything you thought you knew about gravity. Most importantly, remember that while these places may bend the laws of physics, they follow one universal truth: **the best tourist attractions are those that transform confusion into delight**.

Now, if you'll excuse me, I need to sort through my collection of 'gravity-defying' photos and figure out which way is actually up. Though after visiting so many of these mysterious spots, I'm starting to think that 'up' might be more of a suggestion than a rule — much like my sense of equilibrium during these adventures.

Chapter 3

Underground America

Caves, Bunkers, and Secret Nuclear Tourism

Perched at the mouth of Mammoth Cave[1], in Cave City, Kentucky, clutching my trusty flashlight and trying to ignore the fact that my smartphone's battery had just died, I couldn't help but wonder if our ancestors had better sense than to willingly walk into giant holes in the ground. The tour guide's cheerful 'Watch your head!' warning came approximately two seconds after I'd already discovered the cave ceiling's exact height with my forehead, marking the beginning of my adventure into America's underground tourism scene. But today, my throbbing forehead was reminding me that even the most prepared explorer can be humbled by a limestone formation. Welcome to the world of underground tourism, where natural wonders and Cold War relics compete for the title of America's most fascinating subterranean attractions.

Deep beneath the rolling hills and bustling cities lies another America - one carved by water, excavated by miners, or hollowed out by Cold War paranoia. The temperature drops, the darkness thickens, and suddenly your smartphone becomes nothing more than an expensive paperweight. Down here, in the realm of stalactites and blast doors, you'll find yourself navigating a world where nature's patient artistry meets humanity's urgent need for shelter, secrecy, and occasionally, survival.

The underground landscape of America is surprisingly diverse. In Kentucky's Mammoth Cave, ancient limestone passages stretch for more than 400 miles, hosting everything from blind fish to early American graffiti. Meanwhile, in Kansas, decommissioned missile silos have been transformed into luxury bunker condos - perhaps the only real estate market where 'nuclear-proof' is a standard amenity rather than an aspirational upgrade.

My first visit to the Greenbrier Bunker in White Sulphur Springs, West Virginia[2] started with me accidentally joining the wrong tour group - one that was there to sample the resort's afternoon tea service. For fifteen minutes, I couldn't figure out why everyone was more interested in finger sandwiches than fallout shelters. There I was, eagerly pointing out blast doors and asking questions about decontamination showers while my fellow 'tourists' discussed the proper way to hold a teacup. It wasn't until the tour guide politely asked if I was looking for the bunker tour that I realized my mistake. Red-faced, I excused myself from the tea party, but not before pocketing a scone for the road. The real bunker tour proved to be fascinating, though I couldn't help but wonder if those tea-sippers knew they were dining just feet above one of the Cold War's best-kept secrets. The day ended with me getting briefly lost in the massive facility, accidentally finding myself in what turned out to be a modern-day data center, and being politely escorted back to the main tour route by an amused security guard who'd clearly dealt with wandering tourists before.

Category	Details
Name	The Bunker at The Greenbrier (Project Greek Island)
Location	Under The Greenbrier Resort, White Sulphur Springs, West Virginia
Tour Type	Cold War-era declassified bunker tours (90 minutes)
Group Tour Pricing	Adults: $52 each · Youth (10–17): $24 each
Private Tour Pricing	Before 5:00 PM – $1,205.20 (1–25 guests)
	5:00–6:30 PM – $1,766 (1–25 guests)
	6:30–8:00 PM – $1,815 (1–25 guests)
Minimum Age	10 years and above; under-10 not permitted
Reservations	Required; cancel at least 24 hrs in advance
Main Features	112,000 sq ft facility with dorms, hospital, mess hall, blast doors
Accessibility	Contact resort for mobility accommodations
Security Note	No cameras, electronic gear, or bags allowed inside
Parking	Complimentary at the resort
Website	greenbrier.com
Fun Fact	Kept operational for 30 years—even as a glamorous luxury resort above ground.

As we venture deeper into America's subterranean world, remember that underground tourism requires more than just a sense of adventure. **Proper footwear**, **reliable lighting** (preferably not just your phone), and a **healthy respect for both natural formations and man-made structures** are essential. Whether you're exploring limestone labyrinths or Cold War time capsules, there's something profound about descending into spaces where history has literally been preserved in stone - just watch out for those low ceilings. They have a way of making lasting impressions.

Natural Wonders and Cave Tourism: Exploring America's Most Impressive Underground Systems

Deep beneath America's surface lies a world that makes your average basement renovation look like child's play. Instead of storage boxes and forgotten exercise equipment, you'll find cathedral-sized rooms carved by water over millions of years, crystalline formations that sparkle like nature's own chandelier store, and passages that would make a master maze-designer jealous.

My first serious cave expedition taught me a crucial lesson about underground photography - your fancy camera means nothing when you can barely see your hand in front of your face. I'd spent hours researching the perfect settings for low-light shots in Mammoth Cave, only to discover that cave darkness isn't just dark - it's an entirely different species of darkness that devours light like a hungry teenager at an all-you-can-eat buffet.

The natural chambers of **Carlsbad Caverns**[3] , in Guadalupe Mountains, New Mexico, feel less like rooms and more like the inside of a giant geologic jewelry box. The formations create such fantastical shapes that my brain kept trying to assign them familiar names - 'that one looks like my aunt's cat,' or 'pretty sure that's exactly how my leftovers looked last week.' The cave's Natural Entrance trail descends about 750 feet, which is roughly equivalent to climbing down a 75-story building, except the staircase was designed by nature while it was feeling particularly creative.

Category	Details
Name	Carlsbad Caverns National Park
Location	Guadalupe Mountains, near Carlsbad, New Mexico, USA
Type of Attraction	Natural Limestone Cavern System / National Park
Established as Park	1930 (discovered by Jim White in 1898)
Main Features	Giant underground chambers, stalactites/stalagmites, Bat Flight program
Size	Over 119 known caves; Big Room ≈ ~8.2 acres (largest in North America)
Tour Options	Self-guided (Big Room, Natural Entrance) and Ranger-led tours (reservations required)
Opening Hours	Visitor Center: 8:00 AM – 5:00 PM (Cave entry closes at 2:30 PM)
Entry Fees (2025)	Adults (16+): $15 · Kids (≤15): Free · America the Beautiful Pass: Accepted
Additional Fees	Guided tours: $8–$20 depending on route (pre-booking highly recommended)
Accessibility	Big Room is wheelchair-accessible via elevator
Best Time to Visit	Spring or fall for mild temps and fewer crowds
Extra Attractions	Evening bat flights (May–October), scenic desert hiking trails
Website	nps.gov/cave
Fun Fact	The "Big Room" is so vast you could fit six football fields inside it!

In **Virginia's Luray Caverns**[4], I witnessed something truly unique - the **Great Stalacpipe Organ**. Imagine someone looking at ancient rock formations and thinking, 'You know what these need? A good tuning.' The result is an instrument that turns the cave itself into a giant geological xylophone. The sound resonates through the chambers like some sort of underground cathedral choir, though I had to resist the urge to request 'Stairway to Heaven.'

The real magic of cave exploration isn't just in the grand chambers or spectacular formations - it's in the little moments of discovery.

- When your headlamp catches a tiny crystal just right, and suddenly you're seeing colors that seem impossible in the darkness.

- When the absolute silence of a cave is broken only by the steady drip of water that's been crafting these spaces drop by patient drop for longer than humans have walked the Earth.

Category	Details
Name	Luray Caverns
Location	Luray, Virginia, USA (Shenandoah Valley)
Type of Attraction	Commercial Limestone Cave System / Natural Wonder
Discovered	1878
Main Features	Giant stalactites and stalagmites, mirror pools, Great Stalacpipe Organ
Tour Style	Self-paced guided tours (audio + staff in cave), ~1.25 miles walking
Opening Hours	Daily, 9:00 AM - 6:00 PM (year-round)
Tickets (2025)	Adults: ~$32 · Kids (6–12): ~$16 · Under 6: Free
Combo Attractions	Includes Car & Carriage Caravan Museum, Toy Town Junction, Luray Valley Museum
Accessibility	Cave path is paved; mostly accessible, but call ahead for mobility needs
Best Time to Visit	Spring or fall (milder temps and fewer crowds)
Temperature Inside	Constant ~54°F (12°C) year-round
Website	luraycaverns.com
Fun Fact	Home to the **Great Stalacpipe Organ** — the world's largest musical instrument, playing tones by tapping stalactites!

Wind Cave in South Dakota[5] showcases rare boxwork formations that look like someone installed the world's most intricate ceiling tiles. These delicate honeycomb patterns are so abundant here that they make up about 95% of all known boxwork formations in the world. The cave got its name from the barometric winds at its entrance, though don't expect to find any underground tornadoes - it's more like nature's version of a very gentle air conditioning system.

One thing you quickly learn when exploring caves is that your senses adapt in unexpected ways.

- The darkness becomes more than just an absence of light - it develops texture and depth.

- The constant temperature (usually around 55°F) starts to feel normal, making the outside world seem bizarrely warm or cold in comparison.

- Even the subtle scents of limestone and mineral-rich water become distinct and recognizable.

Category	Details
Name	Wind Cave National Park
Location	Near Hot Springs, South Dakota, USA
Type of Attraction	National Park / Limestone Cave System / Prairie Wildlife Preserve
Established as Park	1903 — 7th U.S. National Park & 1st cave designated as such
Discovered by Settlers	1881 (Lakota Sioux knew it long before)
Main Features	Rare **boxwork formations**, frostwork, and cave popcorn
Cave Length	Over 160 miles explored — one of the longest in the world
Tour Options	Ranger-led only: Natural Entrance, Fairgrounds, Garden of Eden, Candlelight, etc.
Opening Hours	Visitor Center: 8:00 AM – 4:30 PM (varies by season); tours require tickets
Tour Fees (2025)	$10–$17 per person depending on tour; America the Beautiful Pass honored
Surface Features	Prairie hikes, bison, elk, prairie dogs, scenic drives
Accessibility	Limited accessible tour routes; contact park for details
Best Time to Visit	Late spring or early fall for mild weather and wildlife viewing
Temperature Inside	Constant ~53°F (12°C)
Website	nps.gov/wica
Fun Fact	Home to **95% of the world's known boxwork**, a honeycomb-like cave formation found almost nowhere else!

Fair warning to those venturing underground: caves have a peculiar effect on human behavior. Perfectly rational people suddenly feel compelled to name every formation they see ('That's definitely Elvis's profile!'), and otherwise coordinated individuals transform into clumsy giants trying to navigate narrow passages without becoming part of the cave's permanent collection. Just remember - if you do bump your head, the echoes will ensure everyone in your tour group knows about it.

For the photographers out there:

- Yes, you should absolutely bring your camera.

- Accept that cave photography is its own special challenge.

- That beautiful formation might look like it's glowing with otherworldly light in person, but your camera will probably capture what appears to be a very convincing photo of absolutely nothing.

- The key is patience, proper equipment, and a willingness to take 47 shots of the same formation until you get one that captures even a fraction of what your eyes are seeing.

These underground spaces remind us that some of America's most impressive architecture wasn't built by human hands at all. They're natural time capsules, preserving millions of years of Earth's history in stone, and they're still being shaped today, one drop of water at a time. Just remember to duck when the guide tells you to - those calcium deposits have been working on their masterpiece for far too long to appreciate your forehead's contribution to the artwork.

Cold War Relics: Converted Missile Silos and Government Bunkers

I never thought I'd find myself 100 feet underground, standing in what was once a launch control center for nuclear missiles, debating the aesthetics of 1960s government-issue furniture with a retired Air Force officer turned tour guide. Yet here I was at the Titan Missile Museum near Tucson, watching him lovingly pat a vintage control panel while explaining how the olive drab color scheme was chosen specifically to calm the nerves of crews tasked with potentially ending civilization.

The museum, the last remaining Titan II site of the 54 that once dotted America like a particularly lethal connect-the-dots puzzle, offers something you won't find at your typical tourist attraction - the chance to get up close and personal with a deactivated nuclear missile. The guides are quick to emphasize the 'deactivated' part, usually right after someone nervously asks about the big pointy thing still aimed at the sky.

Descending those 55 steps into the bunker feels like traveling back in time, except instead of dinosaurs or knights in shining armor, you're surrounded by Cold War technology that somehow manages to be both impressively advanced and endearingly obsolete. The air down here has a distinct quality - a mix of aged concrete, vintage electronics, and what I can only describe as an eau de military-industrial complex.

The acoustic properties of these underground facilities are fascinating. Every footstep echoes with governmental authority, and whispers bounce off blast-hardened walls in ways that would make a cathedral jealous. During my visit, I dropped my pen and the resulting clang reverberated for so long, I'm pretty sure it registered on seismic monitors in neighboring states.

Category	Details
Name	Titan Missile Museum
Location	Green Valley, Arizona (about 30 mins south of Tucson)
Type of Attraction	Cold War Museum / Decommissioned Missile Silo
Established as Museum	1986 (silo was active from 1963–1982)
Main Features	103-foot-tall **Titan II ICBM**, underground launch control center, blast doors
Tour Options	Surface tours, guided silo tours, extended and private tours available
Tour Duration	45 minutes to 1 hour (depending on tour type)
Opening Hours	Daily, 9:30 AM – 5:00 PM (last tour at 4:00 PM)
Admission (2025)	Adults: ~$16 · Seniors/Military: ~$15 · Kids (5–12): ~$12 · Under 5: Free
Accessibility	Above-ground exhibits are accessible; underground areas have stairs only
Security Note	No large bags or backpacks; photos allowed (except where posted)
Special Programs	Moonlight tours, overnight STEM experiences, launch simulations
Website	titanmissilemuseum.org
Fun Fact	It's the only **Titan II missile silo** in the U.S. preserved and open to the public!

Minuteman Missile National Historic Site

At the **Minuteman Missile National Historic Site**[6] in South Dakota, the Delta-09 silo sports a glass ceiling that lets you peer down at a deactivated Minuteman II missile. It's probably the only place where you can safely take a selfie with a nuclear missile without triggering an international incident. The preserved launch control center nearby still bears witness to how crews lived during their 24-hour alert shifts, complete with vintage freeze-dried coffee and the kind of chairs that make you appreciate modern ergonomic design.

Category	Details
Name	Minuteman Missile National Historic Site
Location	Near Wall, South Dakota (just off I-90 and near Badlands National Park)
Type of Attraction	Cold War Missile Silo & Control Center / National Historic Site
Established	1999 (Silo active during 1963–1991)
Main Features	**Delta-01** Launch Control Center and **Delta-09** Missile Silo (with glass top)
Visitor Center	Exhibits on Cold War, nuclear arms race, and missile technology
Tour Options	Ranger-led tour of Delta-01 (reservation required); self-guided Delta-09 & Visitor Center
Tour Duration	~45–60 minutes for Delta-01; open hours for other locations
Opening Hours	Daily, 8:00 AM – 4:00 PM (hours may vary seasonally)
Tickets (2025)	Delta-01 Tour: $12 Adults · $8 Youth (6–16) · Free under 6 · Other sites: Free
Accessibility	Delta-09 & Visitor Center: Accessible · Delta-01: Not fully accessible (stairs only)
Best Time to Visit	Spring or early fall — fewer crowds and nice weather
Website	nps.gov/mimi
Fun Fact	One of the only preserved **nuclear missile sites** where you can see the **launch key panel** and an actual decommissioned **missile** right where it once stood ready for launch.

Oscar-Zero Missile Alert Facility

The **Oscar-Zero Missile Alert Facility**[7] in North Dakota feels frozen in time, right down to the ancient coffee maker that probably deserves its own historic designation. The facility maintains that peculiar underground silence that makes you hyper-aware of every creak and groan of the structure. During my tour, the guide demonstrated the blast door's closing mechanism - a sound that could best be described as 'apocalypse-ready.'

Navigating these facilities requires a certain mindset.

- The corridors weren't designed for tourist traffic.

- Architects clearly prioritized nuclear blast protection over visitor comfort.

- Expect steep stairs, narrow passages, and enough low-hanging pipes to make you wish you'd invested in a hockey helmet.

- The temperature stays consistently cool year-round.

Category	Details
Name	Oscar-Zero Missile Alert Facility (O-0 MAF)
Location	4 miles north of Cooperstown, North Dakota
Type of Attraction	Cold War–era Launch Control Center (Missile Alert Facility) with adjacent Missile Silo (November-33)
Managed By	State Historical Society of North Dakota, in partnership with the Friends of Oscar-Zero
Opening History	Opened to public tours in 2009 after state acquisition in 2008
Tour Includes	22-min orientation video + ~1-hour tour: half topside, half 50 ft below in the underground control center
Admission Fees	Adults: $10 · Youth (6–17): $5 · Children 0–5: Free · Group/student rates: $4 per person · Season/membership discounts available
Hours	· May 16–Labor Day: Daily 10 AM–6 PM · Labor Day–Oct 31 & Apr 1–Memorial Day: Mon/Thu–Sat 10 AM–6 PM, Sun 1–5 PM (closed Tue/Wed) · Nov 1–Mar 31: Tours by appointment only
Accessibility	Wheelchair accessible via freight elevator; potential evacuation by basket if needed
Topside Silo Visit	Free self-guided visit to November-33 Launch Facility (no underground access)
Amenities	Restrooms on-site; small gift shop; no food/drinks allowed on tour
Parking	Free on-site
Fun Fact	The underground crew lounge includes a tropical beach mural—talk about nuclear chill vibes!

The transformation of these sites from ultra-classified military installations to tourist attractions is a testament to how quickly history can pivot. Where armed guards once stood, now stand gift shops selling missile-shaped keychains and 'I survived the Cold War' t-shirts. The same bunkers that were built to withstand nuclear armageddon now struggle with the far more mundane challenge of maintaining adequate Wi-Fi coverage for social media-hungry visitors.

What strikes me most about these places is how they capture the very human element of the Cold War. Behind all the military jargon and impressive technology were regular people:

- Working 24-hour shifts underground

- Playing cards during quiet moments

- Complaining about the quality of the coffee

The preserved crew quarters tell stories of monotony punctuated by moments of intense stress - a bit like modern air travel, but with the fate of humanity potentially hanging in the balance.

For the claustrophobic among us (myself included), these sites require some mental preparation. The spaces can be confining, and there's something uniquely unsettling about being in a facility designed to survive the end of the world. But that's part of what makes these places so fascinating - they're physical reminders of a time when humanity built elaborate underground cities just in case we decided to destroy all the above-ground ones.

Visiting these sites offers more than just a history lesson - it's a visceral reminder of how close we came to using these facilities for their intended purpose. The guides often point out that every mundane detail, from the thickness of the blast doors to the redundancy of the communication systems, was designed with nuclear war in mind. It's sobering to realize that the same rooms now filled with curious tourists were once occupied by people prepared to launch missiles that could have changed the course of human history.

If you plan to visit:

- Wear comfortable shoes with good traction (missile silo floors weren't designed for fashion)

- Bring a light jacket (nuclear bunkers maintain a constant cool temperature)

- Be prepared for stairs - lots of stairs

- And remember: when your guide says 'watch your head,' they're not making a

suggestion

Underground Tourism Safety: A Guide to Not Becoming a Cautionary Tale

I'll never forget the day I learned why underground safety protocols exist. There I was, deep in Jewel Cave, South Dakota[8], when my backup flashlight batteries decided to stage a revolt. My primary light had already given up the ghost an hour earlier, and I found myself doing an embarrassing shuffling dance in the darkness while my tour guide - who'd specifically told us to bring three light sources - tried not to sound too smug about having extra batteries handy.

The underground world doesn't tolerate hubris or poor planning. Mother Nature spent millions of years carving out these spaces, and she didn't install safety railings or emergency exits along the way. While most commercial caves and underground attractions are well-maintained and regularly inspected, they still deserve a healthy dose of respect and preparation.

Let's talk gear:

Your fashion-forward spelunking outfit needs to prioritize function over Instagram aesthetics. Those cute ballet flats might work for brunch, but underground they're about as useful as roller skates in quicksand.

Your underground adventure kit should include:

- A reliable flashlight with extra batteries (or better yet, two flashlights)

- Closed-toe shoes with good grip

- A light jacket (caves maintain a constant cool temperature)

- Water (dehydration happens underground too)

- Basic first-aid supplies

- Any necessary medications

The physical environment underground presents unique challenges. My first time exploring a lava tube, I discovered that 'watch your head' wasn't just friendly advice - it was a survival mantra. The ceiling height would change without warning, and the dark rock made spotting these changes about as easy as finding a black cat in a coal mine at midnight.

Health awareness is crucial. The combination of cool temperatures, humidity, and physical exertion can be deceptive.

- You might not feel like you're sweating, but your body is working hard.

- Listen to your body. Speak up if something feels off.

- Tour guides would much rather help early than organize a rescue.

Additional considerations for military installations and bunkers:

- These facilities weren't designed for comfort.

- Expect steep stairs, narrow corridors, and industrial-grade everything.

- If claustrophobic or mobility-limited, check with the site for accessibility options.

Psychological preparation matters. Some people find these spaces unnervingly confining; others discover peace in the darkness.

During a tour of **Mammoth Cave**, I watched a fully grown man have a panic attack when our guide demonstrated true cave darkness by turning off all lights. It's essential to know your limits and communicate them clearly.

Pay attention to your guide's instructions.

- 'Stay on the marked path' isn't limiting your adventure; it's keeping you safe.

- Barriers around delicate formations protect creations older than civilization.

Environmental awareness is essential.

- Some caves can contain elevated gas levels.

- Tours have time limits for safety reasons, not just guide convenience.

- Water dripping from ceilings may look clear but may contain minerals.

- Some formations are sharp enough to damage clothing.

- Echoes can signal low ceilings ahead.

The goal is to explore safely, not to become the subject of next week's rescue drill. By following guidelines and staying aware, your underground trip will be a highlight—not a cautionary tale.

The Final Ascent

Emerging from the depths of America's underground attractions feels a bit like being born again - if birth involved climbing several hundred stairs while nursing a bruised forehead and carrying a camera full of mostly black photos. These subterranean spaces, whether shaped by nature's patient hand or carved out by Cold War paranoia, offer more than just a unique perspective on American history - they provide a glimpse into our collective fascination with what lies beneath our feet.

The limestone labyrinths of our natural cave systems tell stories written in rock over millions of years, while converted missile silos and government bunkers preserve tales of a time when the threat of nuclear war sent us burrowing into the earth like particularly anxious prairie dogs with military-grade furniture. Each site offers its own distinct flavor of underground adventure, from the sublime natural acoustics of cave chambers to the sobering reality of blast doors designed to withstand the apocalypse.

As I've learned through countless underground expeditions (and several unplanned encounters with low ceilings), the key to enjoying these attractions is equal parts preparation and perspective. **Bring reliable lighting, wear sturdy shoes, and pack a healthy sense of humor** - you'll need all three when you're fifty feet below ground and your tour guide starts telling geological dad jokes that have been fossilizing since the Pleistocene.

Whether you're marveling at ancient limestone formations or contemplating Cold War history in a former missile command center, remember that these underground spaces offer something increasingly rare in our modern world: a chance to disconnect, quite literally, from the surface noise of daily life.

Just watch your step, mind your head, and remember - if you do bump into something in the dark, there's a good chance it's been there for a few million years longer than you have.

Chapter 4

Extraterrestrial Encounters

UFO Hotels, Alien Fresh Jerky, and Desert Conspiracy Tours

T HEY SAY THE TRUTH is out there, but I'm pretty sure it's selling beef jerky somewhere along Highway 375 in Nevada. As your self-appointed guide to the weird and wonderful world of extraterrestrial tourism, I've spent countless hours chasing down every UFO-themed motel and alien-inspired roadside attraction between Area 51 and Roswell, all in the name of thorough research (and questionably flavored snack foods). From Area 51 to Roswell's infamous crash site, America's Southwest has become a mecca for those seeking close encounters of the weird kind. In my quest to experience every alien-themed attraction this side of the Milky Way, I've discovered that extraterrestrial tourism is less about actual UFO sightings and more about the delightfully eccentric humans who've built an entire culture around the possibility of visitors from above.

Wandering through the dusty expanse of Nevada's Extraterrestrial Highway (State Route 375), I've come to appreciate how this 98-mile stretch of asphalt has evolved into something far more significant than just a remote road. The highway cuts through terrain so desolate that your car radio picks up frequencies that sound more like interplanetary communications than local stations. Each year, thousands make the pilgrimage here, their cars loaded with cameras and coolers full of cosmic-themed energy drinks, hoping to witness something extraordinary while sampling questionably flavored beef jerky from alien-themed gift shops.

But beyond the well-known hotspots lies a fascinating network of extraterrestrial attractions that most tourists never discover. Tucked away in desert towns and along forgotten backroads, you'll find everything from homemade UFO observatories constructed from salvaged satellite dishes to surprisingly sophisticated research centers. There's something undeniably compelling about these places where the lines between science fiction and tourism blur into a shimmering desert mirage, punctuated by the glow of neon signs shaped like flying saucers.

What makes these destinations truly special isn't just their otherworldly themes — it's the passionate people who maintain them. Take Bob at the UFO Watchtower in Hooper, Colorado, who can tell you the exact timestamp of every unexplained light he's documented over the past decade. Or the folks at the Atomic Museum in Las Vegas, who somehow manage to connect every exhibit to the possibility of extraterrestrial technology. These dedicated individuals have created more than just tourist stops; they've built communities where believers, skeptics, and the merely curious can come together to ponder our place in the cosmos.

In this chapter, we'll investigate America's extraterrestrial tourism galaxy, from serious research facilities to gloriously kitschy gift shops. You'll learn about:

- The best times to visit these cosmic destinations (**hint: the truth is easier to spot after sunset**)

- How to plan your own close encounters

- And most importantly, where to find the best alien-themed snacks in the solar system

Pack your tinfoil hat and charge your camera batteries —we're about to venture into the heart of America's weirdest tourism frontier.

Alien-Themed Accommodations: From UFO-Shaped Hotels to Desert Motels

If you've ever dreamed of sleeping inside a flying saucer without the hassle of actual alien abduction, you're in luck. America's desert highways are dotted with cosmic crash pads that range from charmingly rustic to ambitiously futuristic. I've spent countless nights in these otherworldly accommodations, each offering its own unique take on extraterrestrial hospitality.

The Little A'Le'Inn in Rachel, Nevada stands as the crown jewel of alien accommodation, though **'jewel' might be overselling it a bit**. This family-owned establishment feels more like a mining camp than the Hilton, but that's precisely its charm. The five simple rooms share bathrooms and come equipped with the basics: bed, TV, and a VCR that's probably old enough to have recorded the original Roswell incident. Yet it's in the common areas where the real magic happens — the ceiling decorated with countless dollar bills left by visitors, each scrawled with messages to potential extraterrestrial visitors. The bar serves their signature **Alien Burger** and a surprisingly decent **Alien Amber Ale**, best enjoyed while swapping UFO stories with fellow travelers.

During my last stay, I witnessed a fascinating cultural exchange between a skeptical physics professor and a group of true believers who'd driven all the way from Maine in a van covered in hand-painted constellation maps. Their heated debate about propulsion systems lasted well into the night, fueled by those aforementioned Alien Ambers and the kind of camaraderie that only emerges in remote desert outposts where cell service is more theoretical than actual.

The wildly ambitious **UFO Hotel project** in Baker, California represents the future of cosmic lodging. Currently under development by **Luis Ramallo**, the visionary behind **Alien Fresh Jerky**, this $30 million venture promises to transport guests into what feels like an actual spaceship. Planned features include:

- Themed rooms

- An alien-inspired spa (though I'm not entirely sure what alien massage techniques might entail)

- Extraterrestrial wedding facilities for couples wanting to tie the knot in orbit, so

to speak

One crucial tip for any otherworldly accommodation: **always check the weather forecast**. Desert temperature swings can be more dramatic than a History Channel alien documentary, and you'll want to ensure your room's climate control system is up to the task. Many of these places are pet-friendly, though it's worth calling ahead — the last thing you need is your German Shepherd being mistaken for a Chupacabra.

These cosmic lodgings serve as more than just novelty accommodations; they're **community gathering spots** where the lines between believer and skeptic blur into a comfortable haze of desert heat and shared wonder. I've witnessed veteran UFO researchers sharing coffee with curious tourists, their conversation drifting from government conspiracies to the best local diners with the kind of easy familiarity that only emerges in places where everyone's a little bit of an outsider.

The desert night sky above these establishments offers its own spectacular show, and many properties have **telescopes available for guest use**. During my stay at one particularly remote motel, the owner — a former NASA engineer with a delightfully dry sense of humor — hosted impromptu astronomy lessons. He'd point out various satellites while casually mentioning which ones he thought might actually be alien observation posts, delivering these theories with such deadpan seriousness that I'm still not entirely sure if he was joking.

Whether you're a dedicated **ufologist** or just someone who enjoys the quirkier side of American tourism, these otherworldly accommodations offer something unique: **a chance to sleep under the same stars that might just be hiding the truth we're all looking for**. And if you don't spot any UFOs during your stay? Well, the thousands of visible stars make for a pretty spectacular consolation prize. Just remember to **bring cash** — alien territory isn't exactly known for reliable credit card machines, and you don't want to end up washing dishes in the galactic diner.

Extraterrestrial Highways and Roadside Attractions

The crown jewel of cosmic road trips has to be **Nevada's State Route 375**[1], better known as the **Extraterrestrial Highway**. This 98-mile stretch of asphalt cuts through some of the most desolate terrain this side of Mars, where your only company might be tumbleweeds, jackrabbits, and the occasional black SUV with government plates pretending not to notice you.

The highway earned its otherworldly designation in **1996**, but locals have been spotting strange lights in the sky since the 1950s. Of course, the road's proximity to **Area 51** might explain some of those sightings — though good luck getting any official confirmation on that. The military installation remained in the realm of conspiracy theory until **2013** when the CIA finally admitted its existence. Even now, they're about as forthcoming with information as a Vulcan at a poker tournament.

During my latest trek down this cosmic corridor, I made the rookie mistake of assuming my car's full tank would easily handle the journey.

Pro tip:

Gas stations along the E.T. Highway are about as common as documented alien autopsies. The desert heat can play tricks on your fuel gauge, and the last thing you want is to end up stranded in an area where your cell phone is more likely to contact Mars than your roadside assistance service.

The highway's crown jewel of peculiarity has to be the **Alien Research Center** near Crystal Springs. Don't let the official-sounding name fool you — it's essentially a gift shop in a Quonset hut, guarded by a three-story-tall metallic alien that looks like it was designed by someone who's watched *Close Encounters* one too many times. The staff, however, are walking encyclopedias of local lore, UFO sightings, and conspiracy theories. They'll happily share stories while helping you pick out the perfect alien-themed shot glass for your collection.

E.T. Fresh Jerky[2] in Hiko deserves special mention, not just for their clever marketing but for proving that even extraterrestrials apparently enjoy dehydrated meat products. The building's exterior is a masterpiece of alien-themed art, featuring everything from cartoon flying saucers to detailed murals of interstellar landscapes. Inside, you'll find an impressive array of jerky flavors.

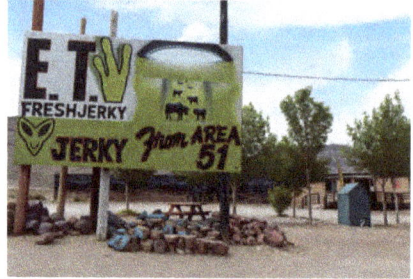

The famous **Little A'Le'Inn**[3] in Rachel serves as both a pit stop and impromptu community center for UFO enthusiasts. During my visit, I witnessed an impromptu gathering of skywatchers sharing photos on their phones while debating whether that strange light on the horizon was a military aircraft, a weather balloon, or something more exotic. The walls are plastered with newspaper clippings, photos, and first-hand accounts of unexplained phenomena, creating an atmosphere that's part diner, part *X-Files* archive.

Perhaps the most poignant spot along the highway is the **Black Mailbox**[4] — or rather, its replacement. The original mailbox, belonging to a local rancher, became such a popular gathering spot for UFO watchers that it had to be replaced with a more sturdy version. Now it serves as an unofficial message center for the extraterrestrial community, stuffed with letters to cosmic visitors and notes from fellow travelers. It's a testament to the human desire to reach out into the unknown, even if the return address might be a few light-years away.

For the best experience, **time your visit around sunset**. As darkness falls, the desert sky transforms into a glittering canopy that makes even hardened skeptics pause and wonder.

The lack of light pollution creates perfect conditions for stargazing, and the silence is profound enough to hear your own heartbeat — or was that the rhythmic humming of a cloaked spacecraft?

Bring a good camera, preferably one that performs well in low light, and **don't forget extra batteries**. The desert has a way of draining electronics faster than usual — though local conspiracy theorists might suggest more otherworldly explanations for dead batteries near Area 51. A **red flashlight** is essential for preserving your night vision while navigating, and **heavy-duty sunscreen** is crucial during daylight hours. The desert sun shows no mercy, even to aspiring ufologists.

Whether you're a true believer or just someone who enjoys the quirkier side of American road culture, the **Extraterrestrial Highway** offers something unique: a chance to experience the thin line between reality and imagination where the horizon stretches endlessly into the unknown. Just remember to **fill up your gas tank whenever possible**, **pack more water than you think you'll need**, and **keep an open mind**. After all, in a universe as vast as ours, who's to say what's really out there?

Desert Conspiracy Tours and Visitor Centers

The desert has a way of making even the most outlandish theories seem plausible. Maybe it's the heat playing tricks on your mind, or perhaps it's the vast emptiness that makes you ponder life's great mysteries. Whatever the reason, I've found myself on countless conspiracy tours, each one more elaborate than the last, searching for glimpses of government secrets while trying not to get sunburned in places I didn't know could get sunburned.

These tours have evolved into a fascinating subculture of American tourism, where retired military personnel, self-proclaimed whistleblowers, and enthusiastic conspiracy theorists guide visitors through the dusty landscapes of the Southwest. **Adventure Photo Tours** runs what they call '**Area 51 Tours**' from Las Vegas, charging $228 for a full day of exploring the perimeter of America's most notorious secret base. The price includes transportation in air-conditioned SUVs, which feels like a bargain when you're cruising through triple-digit temperatures in the Nevada desert.

During my last Area 51 tour, our guide was a former security contractor who spoke in careful euphemisms about his past work experience. He had an uncanny ability to spot unmarked vehicles on distant hills and could recite the exact specifications of various aircraft that officially don't exist. The highlight came when he pointed out a white pickup truck following our group at a distance, explaining with a knowing smile that we were being 'observed.' Whether it was actually government surveillance or just another tourist in a rental car remains one of the desert's many mysteries.

Desert Wonder Tours[5] exemplifies how this niche industry has matured, offering private excursions that blend historical fact with speculative theory. Operating from various locations including Laughlin and Lake Havasu City, they've mastered the art of making government conspiracies feel accessible. Their van-based tours provide an intimate setting for discussions about everything from reverse-engineered alien technology to underground tunnel networks.

The **visitor centers** along these routes range from professional museums to glorified gift shops, each with its own interpretation of classified history. The **Area 51 Alien Center**, located at the entrance to the Extraterrestrial Highway, serves as both a convenient rest stop and an unofficial museum of conspiracy culture. The walls are covered with newspaper clippings, declassified documents, and firsthand accounts from locals who swear they've seen things that defy explanation.

Dr. Diana Pasulka's observation about the American desert being the perfect canvas for conspiracy theories rings particularly true when you're standing at these remote outposts. The vast expanse of sand and sky creates an environment where the line between possible and impossible becomes remarkably fluid. As one tour guide eloquently put it, *'In the desert, the truth doesn't just sparkle — it shimmers like a mirage.'*

Tips for Planning a Conspiracy Tour Adventure

- **Don't rely on your phone's GPS** – some areas have scrambled signals. Bring **paper maps and a compass**.

- **Pack more water than seems reasonable** – conspiracy hunting is thirsty work.

- **Respect the boundaries** – 'restricted area' signs are enforced, and security personnel are not amused.

Most importantly, **maintain a healthy balance between skepticism and wonder**. The best conspiracy tours aren't about proving or disproving anything — they're about exploring the fascinating space where official history meets local legend, where documented fact dances with wild speculation. In these remote corners of the American Southwest, you might not find all the answers, but you'll certainly discover better questions to ask.

Just remember that the **desert itself is often the most mysterious element** of any conspiracy tour. As the sun sets and the temperature drops, casting long shadows across the landscape, it's easy to understand why this harsh and beautiful environment has become the backdrop for so many of America's favorite mysteries. Whether you're a serious researcher or just someone who enjoys a good government cover-up story, these tours offer something unique: a chance to explore the thin line between known and unknown, all while maintaining a comfortable distance from any actual classified information.

As the sun sets over the peculiar landscape of America's UFO country, I find myself reflecting on the fascinating subculture that's sprung up around our collective cosmic curiosity. From the weathered picnic tables outside the Little A'Le'Inn to the gleaming displays at modern visitor centers, this corner of American tourism represents something uniquely human — **our irrepressible desire to believe in possibilities beyond our understanding**.

What started as a quest to document alien-themed attractions has revealed a **community bound together by wonder and possibility**. The retired military personnel who carefully choose their words when discussing their service near Area 51, the passionate tour guides who can recite UFO sightings by date and location, and the gift shop owners who've turned extraterrestrial enthusiasm into thriving businesses — they're all part of a uniquely American story where **entrepreneurship meets existential questioning**.

The desert itself seems to encourage this blend of **commerce and cosmic contemplation**. Under those vast skies, where the horizon stretches endlessly and the stars shine with startling clarity, even the most hardened skeptic might find themselves wondering about what lies beyond. Perhaps that's why these remote locations have become such powerful magnets for those seeking answers to questions that may not have answers.

For travelers planning their own extraterrestrial expeditions, remember that the real value of these experiences often lies in the **unexpected moments**: the late-night conversations with fellow sky-watchers, the surprisingly profound discussions with local residents, and yes, even the questionably-flavored cosmic snack foods. Pack plenty of water, keep your gas tank full, and **maintain a healthy balance between skepticism and wonder**.

As I pack away my tinfoil hat (handcrafted during an impromptu alien fashion show at a UFO-themed diner) and prepare to leave this corner of conspiracy country, I'm struck by how these destinations represent more than just quirky tourist attractions. They're physical manifestations of humanity's eternal question: **are we alone?** And while I can't claim to have spotted any definitive evidence of extraterrestrial visitors during my travels, I've discovered something equally valuable — **a community of people who've turned that universal uncertainty into something uniquely, wonderfully human**.

So whether you're a dedicated ufologist or just someone who enjoys the quirkier side of American tourism, these cosmic destinations offer something rare and precious: **a chance to embrace the unknown while enjoying some of the best beef jerky this side of the Milky Way**. Just remember to **bring cash** — alien territory isn't exactly known for reliable credit card machines, and you don't want to end up washing dishes in the galactic diner.

Chapter 5

Houses of the Holy Strange

Religious Folk Art and Divine Inspiration

Divine Inspiration in Recyclable Containers

A s I LOOKED IN awe at the towering bottle walls of the Bottle Chapel at Airlie Gardens[1] in Wilmington, North Carolina, I couldn't help but ponder whether divine inspiration can be found in recyclable containers. The sunlight filtering through thousands of colored glass bottles created an otherworldly kaleidoscope effect that made me understand why folk artists so often claim their work comes from a higher power.

Across America, passionate creators have fashioned sacred spaces from the most mundane materials — bottle walls that glow like stained glass, concrete kingdoms built by divine inspiration, and gardens where rust and resurrection intertwine. These DIY devotional sites represent a uniquely American blend of religious fervor, artistic vision, and the unshakeable conviction that God's message can be shared through everything from salvaged car parts to thousands of hand-painted stones.

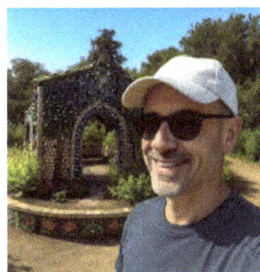

Humble Beginnings and Bold Visions

These unconventional sacred spaces often begin with a simple vision — a dream, a calling, or sometimes just an overwhelming urge to create.

- **Brother Joseph Zoettl** spent nearly 50 years building the Ave Maria Grotto[2] in Alabama, crafting miniature religious buildings from concrete, marbles, and broken dishes.

- **Leonard Knight** spent decades painting Salvation Mountain[3] in the California desert, using thousands of gallons of donated paint to spread his message of love.

Their dedication transforms everyday objects into extraordinary expressions of faith, proving that divine inspiration can work through the most unlikely mediums.

The Creators: A Tapestry of American Spirituality

The creators themselves form a fascinating tapestry of American spirituality.

- Some are ordained ministers who felt called to express their faith through unconventional means.

- Others are self-taught artists who discovered their calling later in life, often after personal hardships or divine revelations.

- Many work in solitude, guided by visions only they can see.

- Others build vibrant communities around their creations, drawing volunteers and believers who help maintain and expand these sacred spaces.

Practical Pilgrimage Tips

I've learned to approach these sites with an open mind and comfortable shoes — you never know when you'll need to climb through a recycled metal archway or navigate a maze of handcrafted biblical scenes. The creators of these spaces often work for decades without blueprints or building permits, guided only by their personal visions and an apparently relaxed interpretation of local zoning laws.

- Some are proud roadside attractions, drawing curious tourists with promises of miracle photo opportunities.

- Others hide down dusty back roads, known only to locals who treat them with a mixture of pride and mild embarrassment, like an eccentric but beloved relative.

A Serendipitous Beginning

My journey through America's folk art sacred spaces began almost by accident. I discovered the Wisconsin Concrete Park[4] on a sweltering Tuesday in July, 2017 when my car's GPS decided that the best route to Minneapolis involved taking me through the small town of Phillips. As I pulled into the parking lot, I was greeted by an army of concrete figures — over 200 of them — created by former lumberjack Fred Smith in his divine quest to preserve local history.

While photographing a particularly impressive concrete angel, I met Martha, the site's elderly volunteer guide, who insisted on showing me every single sculpture while sharing increasingly elaborate theories about their spiritual significance. What started as a quick roadside stop turned into a three-hour tour, complete with Martha's homemade lemonade and detailed explanations of how Smith received his artistic visions. By the time I left, I had a camera full of photos, a notebook full of local legends, and a newfound appreciation for the thin line between artistic inspiration and divine intervention.

Exploring the Chapter Ahead

In this chapter, we'll examine these fascinating monuments to faith and creativity, from the famous **Watts Towers in Los Angeles** to tiny **roadside shrines built from beer cans and broken tiles.**

- We'll meet the devoted caretakers who maintain these spaces.

- We'll learn the unwritten rules of respectful visitation.

- We'll discover how these unconventional expressions of faith have become un-expected pillars of their communities.

Pack your camera, bring an open mind, and please — resist the urge to add your own artistic contributions. These sites may welcome your prayers, but they probably don't need your amateur mosaic work.

Roadside Grottos and Prayer Gardens: America's DIY Sacred Spaces

Driving America's backroads, you'll find sacred spaces tucked between cornfields and behind gas stations, where devoted individuals have transformed ordinary plots into extraordinary sanctuaries. These DIY devotional sites range from elaborate grottos adorned with countless pieces of broken glass to humble prayer gardens where plastic flowers bloom eternally beneath weathered statues of saints.

The Dickeyville Grotto, Wisconsin

The Dickeyville Grotto[5] in Dickeyville, Wisconsin stands as perhaps the most spectacular example of this uniquely American form of devotional folk art. Father Matthias Wernerus spent nearly a decade creating this glittering masterpiece, which looks like what might happen if a religious vision collided with the contents of a magpie's nest. The good Father incorporated everything from glass shards to geodes, costume jewelry to coral fragments, creating intricate mosaics that tell both religious and patriotic stories. Visit at sunrise or sunset when the light catches the crystalline surfaces just right, transforming the entire structure into a kaleidoscope of color and faith.

Ave Maria Grotto, Alabama

Down in Alabama, near Huntsville, Brother Joseph Zoettl's Ave Maria Grotto[6] offers a different take on sacred spaces. Known affectionately as **'Jerusalem in Miniature,'** this four-acre garden contains 125 miniature reproductions of religious structures from around the world. Brother Joseph, standing barely four feet tall himself, spent nearly 70 years crafting these intricate models using concrete, marbles, tiles, and an astonishing array of donated materials. The result is a sprawling garden of tiny architectural wonders that makes you feel like Gulliver touring a sacred Lilliput.

Wonder Cave at the Rudolph Grotto Gardens, Wisconsin

Wisconsin's Wonder Cave at the Rudolph Grotto Gardens[7] offers visitors a particularly immersive experience. Father Philip Wagner, inspired by a pilgrimage to Lourdes, transformed a humble potato field into an extensive complex of shrines and contemplative spaces. The cave itself is actually an above-ground passage lined with religious art and devotional objects, proof that sometimes the most profound journeys happen at ground level. I learned this the hard way when my phone died halfway through the dimly lit passage, leaving me to navigate by touch and faith - mostly faith.

Respecting Sacred Spaces

During my visit to these sites, I've discovered they operate on what I call **'spiritual karma insurance'** - most run on donations, and it feels somehow wrong to stiff a place that's essentially a direct line to the divine. But beyond monetary contributions, these spaces ask for something more valuable: **respect.** These aren't Instagram backdrops or roadside carnival attractions; they're active sites of worship where people come to pray, reflect, and occasionally get lost in wonder caves.

Planning Your Visit

- **Best times to visit:** Early morning or late afternoon, when the light is perfect for photos and the temperatures are more forgiving.

- **Seasonal tips:** Many sites are open year-round, though winter visits require careful navigation of potentially icy paths.

- **Etiquette:** While you might be tempted to add your own artistic contribution to these collective works of faith, **resist the urge.** Your bottle cap mosaic skills, however impressive, are probably not divinely inspired.

A Testament to American Devotion

Each of these sacred spaces tells a story of individual vision and collective faith, where the line between art and devotion blurs into something uniquely American. They remind us that spirituality doesn't always require grand cathedrals or ancient rituals - sometimes it just needs a passionate creator, some recycled materials, and enough concrete to worry the local hardware store. These places aren't just tourist attractions; they're testaments to the human desire to create something larger than ourselves, even if we have to build it one broken tile at a time.

Visionary Architecture: When Faith Meets Folk Art

When divine inspiration meets architectural ambition, the results tend to be gloriously unpredictable. Across America, visionary builders have created structures that defy conventional design wisdom, guided by spiritual callings that apparently didn't include consulting building codes. These architectural marvels range from towering monuments built by lone visionaries to sprawling environments that look like fever dreams rendered in concrete and steel.

Salvation Mountain, California

Take **Salvation Mountain** in Niland, California —
a technicolor testament to what happens when you
give a man named Leonard Knight thousands of gallons of paint and an adobe hill in the desert. This
vibrant piece rises from the dusty landscape like a Dr.
Seuss illustration that found religion, its messages of
universal love visible from startling distances. During
my first visit, I watched as a group of art students
attempted to capture its essence in watercolors, their
frustrated sighs suggesting that some visions simply can't be contained in conventional
mediums.

Watts Towers, Los Angeles

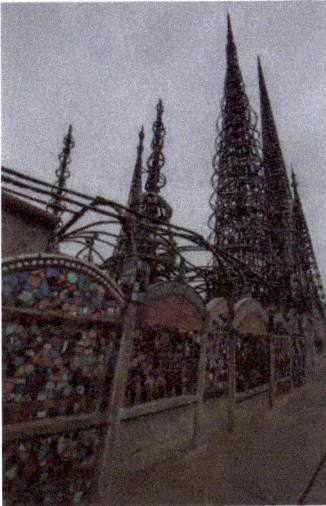

The **Watts Towers**[8] in Los Angeles stand as another
masterpiece of visionary architecture, though their
spiritual nature is more implied than explicit. Simon
Rodia spent 33 years building these soaring spires
from steel rebar, concrete, and whatever caught his
magpie eye. The towers rise like industrial prayer ar-
rows, decorated with a treasury of broken glass, pottery shards, and seashells. On my last visit, I overheard
a child ask their parent why the towers were built.
The parent's response — *"Because sometimes people
just need to build something beautiful"* — might be the
best explanation I've heard yet.

House on the Rock, Wisconsin

The **House on the Rock**[9] in Spring Green, Wisconsin, defies easy categorization — it's
what might happen if religious architecture had a lengthy conversation with a carnival
funhouse. Creator Alex Jordan Jr. built what might be the world's most elaborate man
cave, then kept going until it became something between a spiritual journey and an

episode of *'Hoarders: Architectural Edition.'* The infamous carousel room alone contains 269 carousel creatures (none of them horses) and over 20,000 lights. My attempt to photograph it ended with me lying flat on my back, trying to capture the full scope of this mechanical fever dream while other tourists politely stepped around me.

Bishop Castle, Colorado

In **Bishop Castle**[10], in Pueblo, Colorado, Jim Bishop has spent over 60 years single-handedly constructing a massive castle complex complete with fire-breathing dragon head. What began as a simple stone cottage evolved into a soaring testament to one man's determination to build his own medieval fantasy, despite what local building inspectors might have to say about it. The structure includes wrought iron bridges that sway unnervingly in the wind and towers that reach toward the heavens with more enthusiasm than engineering precision.

Tips for Visiting Visionary Architecture Sites

These places often lack standard tourist amenities — bathrooms might be scarce, gift shops nonexistent, and snack bars nothing more than a distant dream. **Pack accordingly**, and remember that the nearest restaurant might be miles away. But what these sites lack in convenience, they make up for in pure, unfiltered American ingenuity.

- Most locations operate on **donation systems** — contributing supports the continued maintenance of these incredible visions.

- **Photography is usually welcomed,** though tripods might require special permission.

- Do not treat these structures as playgrounds — while they look wild, they're not built for climbing or rough use.

During my visit to Bishop Castle, I watched Jim Bishop himself scaling the towers well into his seventies, proof that some visions demand lifelong dedication.

Practical Advice for Pilgrims of the Unusual

- **Visit early in the day** to avoid heat and crowds.

- **Bring water** and **wear sturdy shoes.**

- **Keep an open mind** — you're not just visiting buildings, you're stepping into someone else's dream made manifest in wood, stone, and determined vision.

Testaments to the Spirit

These architectural outliers remind us that sometimes the most impressive structures come not from prestigious firms but from individuals who heard a calling and answered it with concrete and determination. They stand as testimonies to the human spirit's capacity to create something extraordinary, even if that something occasionally requires warning signs about structural stability.

Sacred Recycling: Found Object Religious Art Installations

The first time I encountered **Howard Finster's Paradise Garden**[11] in Summerville, Georgia, I stood transfixed before a towering chapel made entirely from bicycle parts, hubcaps, and what appeared to be every mirror shard in the state. The late reverend's masterpiece gleamed in the afternoon sun like some kind of recycled revelation, proof that divine inspiration works in mysterious ways — sometimes through old bicycle chains and broken glass.

Salvage Yards as Sacred Ground

Across America, visionary artists have turned salvage yards into sacred spaces, transforming society's castoffs into testaments of faith. These creators don't just see trash — they see raw materials for manifesting their spiritual visions.

- Old bottles become stained glass

- Rusty farm equipment morphs into angels

- Discarded machinery finds new life as religious iconography

In Wisconsin, I met **Ernest Haberland**, who spent thirty years creating his *'Holy Ghost Park'* using materials salvaged from local junkyards. *"God doesn't care if His message comes through gold leaf or old car parts,"* he told me while showing off a Madonna crafted from chrome bumpers and headlights. *"Sometimes the holiest things come from the humblest materials."* There was something undeniably transcendent about how the morning light played across his installations, turning ordinary scrap metal into something extraordinary.

Spiritual Vision Through Found Materials

These sacred recycling sites often spring up in economically challenged areas, where artists work with whatever materials they can find. The resourcefulness is remarkable.

- Devotional sculptures made from old washing machines

- Collections of bottle caps rivaling any recycling center

- Stations of the cross constructed from license plates

- Meditation labyrinths lined with broken pottery and recycled bricks

There's a raw authenticity to these places that you just don't find in conventional religious spaces.

Visiting Tips for Sacred Recycling Sites

- **Outdoor installations:** Check the weather before visiting.

- **Best lighting:** Early morning or late afternoon makes bottle walls glow.

- **Footwear:** Wear good walking shoes — sculpture gardens often involve uneven terrain.

- **Bring water:** Many sites lack amenities.

- **Donation boxes:** Carry cash — most sites rely on visitor contributions.

At **Joe Minter's African Village in America**[12] in Birmingham, Alabama, thousands of found objects tell stories of faith, struggle, and redemption. Minter has transformed his property into a powerful meditation on African American history and spirituality, using everything from old tools to chains. Each piece tells a story, showing how even the rustiest object can preserve memory and truth.

The Art in the Details

The creativity at these sites seems endless. While a giant cross made of automobile grills may be the obvious focal point, the deeper spiritual messages often lie in subtler details:

- The arrangement of colored glass in a bottle wall

- The timing of sunlight illuminating certain pieces

- The hidden symbolism in seemingly random arrangements

These sites require you to **look closer**, not just at the art but at the intent behind it.

Embracing the Unconventional

Some visitors struggle with the unconventional nature of these spaces. They expect religious art to be polished, formal, and expensive. But there's something profoundly moving about faith expressed through humble materials.

- These sites began as **private expressions** of faith

- Today they serve as **accessible sacred art environments**

- The juxtaposition of ordinary objects with sacred themes makes them relatable and grounded

After all, it's difficult to feel intimidated by divine inspiration when it comes in the form of artfully arranged washing machine parts.

Living Works of Faith

What I find most remarkable about these sacred recycling sites is their **ongoing evolution**. Unlike traditional religious spaces, these installations:

- **Grow and change over time**

- **Reflect the living nature of faith**

- **Continue to receive new pieces and rearrangements**

They're dynamic works of devotion — just **watch your step**. Enlightenment shouldn't require a tetanus shot.

A Reflection of American Faith

As I prepare to leave Howard Finster's Paradise Garden, watching the setting sun transform bottle walls into prisms of colored light, I'm struck by how these unconventional sacred spaces embody something quintessentially American. They represent

- A long tradition of **religious freedom**

- The right to express **faith through individual vision**

- Sacredness found in **bottle chapels** and **concrete kingdoms** built by hand

These places remind us that **divine inspiration doesn't discriminate** between materials or methods. Their creators — whether former lumberjacks, retired postal workers, or self-taught visionaries — share a common thread: **the courage to build something extraordinary from ordinary materials**, guided by personal conviction rather than architectural convention.

These sites may not appear in traditional tourist guides, but they offer something increasingly rare: **authentic expressions of faith**, unfiltered by committees or focus groups.

Final Thoughts

What began as my somewhat skeptical exploration of America's religious folk art has evolved into a **profound appreciation** for these sacred spaces and their creators. They stand as testaments not just to faith, but to the **human drive to create something meaningful** from whatever materials life provides.

In an age of mass-produced everything, these handcrafted havens remind us that some-times the most powerful spiritual experiences happen not in polished perfection, but in places where **passion, creativity, and faith collide in wonderfully unexpected ways.**

Chapter 6

Forgotten Theme Parks

Abandoned Dreams and Quirky Comebacks

Wondering if the swing sets still moved on windless nights, I stood at the rusty gates of what was once Lake Shawee Amusement Park[1] in West Virginia. In stark contrast to the overcast sky, the deserted Ferris wheel stood like a giant's long-lost pocket watch, its skeleton frame bearing the weight of vanished summers.

More than simply evoking eerie fantasies, these deserted paradises provide **intimate details** about the lives of the people who previously called them home.

In Lake Shawnee Park, local families still reminisce about summer afternoons spent on the swing sets, their memories now intertwined with the wild grapevines that embrace the metal frames. At Six Flags New Orleans, the watermarks left by Hurricane Katrina serve as somber reminders of nature's raw power, while graffiti artists have transformed weathered walls into vibrant canvases, creating beauty from devastation.

Transformation of Abandoned Spaces

But what truly captivates isn't just the decay - it's the unexpected ways these spaces find new purpose.

Take Rocky Point Park [2]in Rhode Island, where tai chi practitioners now find serenity beneath rusted roller coaster tracks. Every morning, their graceful movements contrast wonderfully with the stark industrial remains, as elderly students master ancient arts where teenagers once screamed through loop-de-loops. The old carousel platform, stripped of its painted horses, has become an impromptu yoga studio during full moon meditation sessions.

Sometimes the most profound transformations happen when we stop trying to recapture the past and instead embrace new possibilities.

Evolution of Abandoned Parks

These parks don't just fade away; they evolve.

- Nature performs its slow reclamation with artistic flair, painting rust patterns on metal and weaving Virginia creeper through chain-link fences.

- Local artists see blank canvases where others see decay, turning crumbling walls into galleries and abandoned pavilions into impromptu performance spaces.

- Even the concrete foundations of dismantled rides find new life as gathering spots for photographers, urban explorers, and those seeking quiet reflection amidst the ruins.

A Call for Respect and Caution

Exploring these places requires equal parts respect and caution.

- Many sit on private property, their structures weathered by decades of exposure to the elements.

- Smart visitors always obtain proper permissions, bring reliable flashlights, and never explore alone.

- The thrill of discovery isn't worth risking a close encounter with tetanus or a sudden fall through rotted floorboards.

These sites deserve to be documented and remembered, but safely and legally.

Digital Era and Enduring Inspiration

As our entertainment landscape continues to shift toward digital experiences and virtual thrills, more parks will inevitably join the ranks of these atmospheric ruins.

Yet in their afterlife, they offer something equally valuable - a chance to witness how communities adapt and evolve. They remind us that nothing truly dies as long as it continues to inspire, whether through art, meditation, or simply serving as a canvas for nature's patient reclamation.

These parks may have stopped selling tickets, but they never stopped telling stories.

When Wilderness Takes Back the Magic Kingdom

Subtle Beginnings of Nature's Return

The first signs are subtle - moss painting abstract murals across forgotten walkways, dandelions pushing through cracks in the pavement with stubborn determination.

At Six Flags New Orleans, I watched an alligator bask lazily where lines once formed for the Mega Zeph roller coaster. The massive wooden coaster now serves as nature's own jungle gym, with stubborn vines climbing ever higher each season. My guide that day, a wildlife photographer named Marcus who's been documenting the park's transformation since Katrina, pointed out a family of raccoons that had converted an old funnel cake stand into their personal penthouse suite.

"They've got better real estate instincts than most humans," he chuckled. **"Prime location, waterfront view."**

Stages of Reclamation

The process of reclamation follows a fascinating pattern that I've observed across dozens of abandoned parks.

- First come the opportunistic plants - those pioneer species that thrive in disturbed environments.

- Then arrive the smaller creatures: birds constructing elaborate nests in defunct ticket booths and spiders spinning webs between silent carousel horses that once carried laughing children.

- Finally, larger wildlife moves in, transforming these former temples of human amusement into thriving ecosystems.

A Different Kind of Congregation

During my visit to Heritage USA[3] in South Carolina, I discovered how quickly nature can erase our grandest ambitions.

The former Christian theme park, once America's third most-visited attraction, now hosts a different kind of congregation. Deer graze peacefully in what was once the main parking lot, while former water slides peek through dense underbrush like ancient Mayan ruins.

The property's current caretaker, Jim, shared stories of finding black bears investigating the remains of the amphitheater. **"Sometimes late in the evening,"** he told me, **"you'll hear coyotes howling from the top of what used to be the Noah's Ark play structure. Seems fitting somehow."**

Accidental Urban Ecology Labs

These spaces have become accidental laboratories of urban ecology.

- At Kentucky Kingdom's abandoned sections, botanists have documented rare native species returning to land that was once covered in concrete and artificial landscaping.

- Lake Shawnee Park in West Virginia now serves as an unofficial wildlife sanctuary, its rusted rides providing perfect perches for hawks and owls.

- The lake that once hosted pedal boats now supports a thriving population of herons and water-loving creatures.

Lessons in Preparedness

For those seeking to witness this transformation firsthand, preparation is crucial.

I learned this lesson the hard way at Lake Shawnee, when what I thought was solid ground turned out to be a moss-covered pool cover. My camera survived the adventure better than my dignity, and Marcus still brings up the incident whenever we cross paths.

Structural integrity decreases as vegetation increases - that picturesque ivy-covered building might look stable, but it's probably not the best place to set up your tripod.

Stories Behind the Abandonment

Each abandoned park tells a unique story of economic shifts and changing entertainment tastes.

- Dogpatch USA[4] in Arkansas closed due to shifting vacation patterns and competition from larger parks.

- Yet its new life as a natural area provides different kinds of value - from wildlife habitat to watershed protection.

- Some properties exist in legal limbo between private ownership and public access, while others have found new purpose through community initiatives.

In Kentucky, I met a group of conservationists working to transform an abandoned park into a dedicated nature preserve, proving that sometimes the best future for these spaces embraces their wild second act.

Every rusted roller coaster wrapped in kudzu and every concrete foundation split by tree roots reminds us that nature always gets the final say.

Perhaps there's poetry in how these parks, once built to help humans escape from reality, now serve as perfect examples of reality's unstoppable force. They've become living museums where you can witness the gradual victory of wilderness over our carefully constructed illusions of control.

Yet there's beauty in this transformation that goes beyond mere decay.

Where children once lined up for cotton candy, foxes now den beneath weathered concession stands. The screams of thrill-seekers have been replaced by the calls of nesting birds.

Nature doesn't waste time mourning what was lost - it simply gets busy creating something new from what remains.

From Thrills to Chills: America's Most Hauntingly Beautiful Abandoned Parks

The first time I stepped into Chippewa Lake Park[5] in Ohio, the silence hit me harder than any roller coaster drop ever could. Where carousel music once played, wind whispered through maple saplings growing straight through rusted ride platforms. The park's iconic Ferris wheel stood frozen in time, its skeleton serving as nature's most elaborate trellis. A determined oak tree had grown right through the center, its branches reaching through the spokes like fingers through a spider's web.

These abandoned parks carry emotional weight far beyond their physical remains. At Lake Shawnee in West Virginia, I met Tom, a former maintenance worker who spent his teenage summers painting the very rides that now stand as rustic sculptures. **"We weren't just maintaining machines,"** he told me, voice thick with emotion, **"we were keeping dreams running."** The park closed in 1966 after two tragic accidents and struggled through several failed reopening attempts, each leaving its own layer of history and heartache.

The stories behind these closures are as varied as the parks themselves. Dogpatch USA in Arkansas didn't fall victim to just changing entertainment tastes – it struggled with the brutal combination of rising insurance costs, the gas crisis of the 1970s, and a shift in family vacation patterns that favored larger destination parks. When I visited last spring, I found Johnny, the groundskeeper, tending to the property not because he's paid to (he isn't) but because he believes these places deserve dignity even in decline.

Perhaps the most sobering stop on my abandoned park tour was Six Flags New Orleans. Hurricane Katrina transformed this once-vibrant park into an accidental monument to nature's raw power, but the real story lies in the community's relationship with the ruins. Local artists have turned weathered walls into canvases, creating beauty from devastation. I found a waterlogged park map from 2005, its cheerful cartoon illustrations still visible beneath a layer of grime, marking attractions that now exist only in memory and maintenance records.

The Three R's of Responsible Ruin Photography

Exploring these places requires more than just curiosity and a decent camera. During my research, I've developed what I call the **Three R's of Responsible Ruin Photography**:

1. **Research** – verify if visits are permitted

2. **Respect** – both property rights and personal safety

3. **Resist** – the urge to take souvenirs; let the memories and photos be enough

Many sites are actively monitored, and trespassing charges can turn your urban exploration adventure into an expensive lesson in property law.

More Than Ruins: Cultural Time Capsules

But beyond the decay and danger, these abandoned parks offer something uniquely valuable – they're time capsules of American leisure history. Each rusted ride and crumbling concession stand tells a story about how we once spent our free time and disposable income. The evolution from small, family-owned parks to corporate entertainment empires is written in their remains.

At Joyland[6] in Wichita, Kansas, the morning sun filtering through broken windows creates light shows that no designer could have planned. Nature's slow reclamation project has transformed mundane structures into haunting sculptures that would look right at home in a modern art museum. The old wooden roller coaster, its track warped by decades of Kansas weather, stands as a ghostly reminder of simpler thrills.

Some parks find unexpected second lives. Rocky Point in Rhode Island has been partially reclaimed as a public space, where joggers now trace paths once lined with game booths and food stands. The site's transformation from private amusement park to public gathering space offers hope that these places can evolve rather than simply decay.

As I stood at Lake Shawnee's entrance one final time, watching the sunset paint the rusted rides in shades of gold, I realized these parks aren't really abandoned – they're just entertaining a different kind of visitor now. Whether they serve as catalysts for reflection, canvases for artists, or sanctuaries for local wildlife, they continue to spark wonder in those who venture past their weathered gates. Sometimes the most profound experiences come not from the height of a roller coaster drop but from standing in its shadow, listening to the stories whispered by the wind through its empty track.

Phoenix Parks: Abandoned Attractions Finding New Purpose

In Phoenix, where the sun bakes memories into permanent shadows, abandoned amusement parks tell stories of **reinvention** rather than decay. I discovered this firsthand during my exploration of **Legend City's** remains, where corporate cubicles now occupy spaces that once echoed with roller coaster screams and carnival music. The transformation feels both jarring and perfectly Phoenix – a city that's made an art form out of reinventing itself.

Legend City: Ambition and Adaptation

Legend City's[7] saga reads like a masterclass in American entertainment economics. Opening in 1963 with Louis E. Crandall's ambitious vision of creating "Arizona's Disneyland," the park managed the impressive feat of declaring bankruptcy within six months. Walking through what's now an office complex, I met Mike, a security guard who'd worked at Legend City during its final days under Mitsubishi's ownership.

"Try explaining to Japanese executives why we needed a mechanical bull named Dusty," he chuckled, sharing stories of cultural confusion and corporate compromise that finally led to the park's closure in 1983.

Cracker Jax to Community Garden

The emotional resonance of these transformed spaces runs deeper than mere nostalgia. At **CrackerJax Family Fun Park's[8]** former site, I found a thriving community garden where go-kart tracks once carved through the desert soil. Maria, one of the garden's organizers, showed me how they'd repurposed old game booth foundations as raised planters.

"The irrigation system still had good bones," she explained, proud of how they'd turned entertainment infrastructure into food production. **"Though we did find a lot of lost tokens while preparing the soil."**

Compton Terrace: From Rock Concerts to Farmers' Markets

These reimagined spaces often find surprising new purpose through grassroots initiatives. The former **Compton Terrace[9] amphitheater**, where rock concerts once shook the desert nights, now hosts one of Phoenix's largest farmers' markets. I watched vendors set up their stalls in the shadow of old speaker towers, the concrete terracing that once held screaming fans now providing perfect displays for local produce. A former roadie-turned-organic farmer told me he sometimes swears he can still hear echoes of Metallica when the wind hits the remaining structure just right.

Preservation Through Progress

The successful reinvention of these spaces requires a delicate balance between preservation and progress. At the site of the former **Paradise Valley Speedway**, architects incorporated elements of the old racetrack into a new mixed-use development. Walking the grounds, you can still trace the original curve of the track in the landscaping, while salvaged signage serves as public art. It's a thoughtful approach to development that honors the site's history while creating something new.

Safety in the Desert

For those interested in exploring these transformed attractions, remember that the desert demands respect even in urban settings.

- Bring more water than you think you need

- Wear sturdy shoes (tetanus shots aren't included in the admission price to abandoned lots)

- Always secure proper permissions before visiting

Phoenix's Reinvention Ethos

The story of Phoenix's abandoned attractions isn't one of failure, but of **evolution**. While Legend City tried to capture the spirit of the Old West, its transformation into office space perhaps captures an even more authentic American tradition – our endless cycle of reinvention.

These spaces remind us that sometimes the most valuable legacy isn't in preserving the past exactly as it was but in finding creative ways to give it new life. Behind every repurposed theme park and reimagined entertainment venue, there's a community making conscious choices about how to honor their history while building something new. It's a uniquely Phoenix approach to preservation – one that understands the best way to remember our past might be to give it a future.

Evolving Memories: Parks in Transition

The stories of these abandoned parks reveal something deeper than just nostalgic decay or haunting beauty – they show us how communities adapt, heal, and reimagine spaces that once defined their summers.

- From the **tai chi practitioners** finding zen beneath Rocky Point's silent coasters

- To the **wildlife reclaiming** Lake Shawnee's grounds

These parks have evolved from destinations of manufactured thrills to places of **organic wonder and unexpected renewal**.

The economic forces that closed these parks tell complex tales about changing entertainment tastes, rising insurance costs, and shifts in how Americans spend their leisure time. Yet in their afterlife, these spaces offer something equally valuable – they become living laboratories where nature experiments with reclamation, artists find inspiration in decay, and communities discover new ways to use familiar spaces.

- The rusted Ferris wheel that once carried giggling children now frames sunrise yoga sessions

- The wooden coaster that thrilled teenagers now provides shelter for nesting birds and serves as nature's most elaborate trellis

Urban Exploration With Purpose

For those drawn to explore these transformed kingdoms, remember that **respect must guide every step**. These aren't just abandoned properties; they're repositories of memories both joyful and tragic, and their structures grow more delicate with each passing season.

- Proper permissions

- Safety precautions

- A deep appreciation for the stories these places hold

These are essential companions on any urban exploration adventure.

New Stories in Old Places

The real thrill isn't in defying "No Trespassing" signs but in discovering how these once-bustling attractions have found **unexpected new purpose**.

Perhaps that's the most profound lesson these abandoned parks teach us: that **endings rarely mark true conclusions**. Sometimes they're just intermissions in a longer show, where nature takes center stage and communities rewrite the script.

In the quiet spaces between rusted rides and overgrown paths, we find something more meaningful than carnival barkers and cotton candy. We find stories of **resilience, transformation**, and the strange beauty that emerges when we simply step back and let time work its particular magic.

These parks may have stopped selling tickets, but they never stopped creating memories; they just changed the kind of memories they make.

Chapter 7

Museum of the Bizarre

Collections That Defy Description

A T THE DEVIL'S ROPE Museum[1] in McLean, Texas, a meticulously arranged display of 1,506 different types of barbed wire left me wondering what motivated someone to dedicate their life to collecting twisted metal. It's a question that would follow me through countless peculiar museums across America, where passionate curators have transformed their obsessions into surprisingly engaging exhibitions that range from the mundane to the magnificent. These passionate preservationists come in all varieties, from the retired history teacher who spent 40 years collecting vintage toasters to the former Wall Street executive who now curates America's largest collection of vacuum cleaners. They're united by an infectious enthusiasm that can turn even the most mundane objects into fascinating artifacts with stories spanning decades or even centuries.

The Personal Touch: Passionate Curators and Their Stories

Consider Mike, the eccentric curator at the Kansas Barbed Wire Museum[2], who once successfully defended his museum in court when a visiting artist tried to sue after getting tangled in an "interactive" display. Mike now proudly tells this story during every tour, pointing out

the "legally problematic" exhibit while explaining
how this particular strand of barbed wire helped shape the American West. His eyes light
up as he describes the subtle differences between the "Winner" and "Glidden" barbed wire
patterns of 1874, making what could be a mundane topic feel like a thrilling detective
story.

These museums often operate on shoestring
budgets, powered by volunteer staff and donations from equally obsessed collectors. The International Towing and Recovery Museum[3] in
Chattanooga stands as a testament to this dedication, where retired tow truck drivers volunteer
their time to maintain vintage vehicles and share
stories of legendary recoveries. During my visit, I met Jim, a former driver who could
recite the technical specifications of every vehicle on display while simultaneously telling
hair-raising stories about rescuing cars from precarious mountain ledges. His enthusiasm
was so contagious that I found myself genuinely fascinated by the engineering evolution
of tow trucks - something I never thought would interest me.

Embracing the Absurd: What Awaits in This Chapter

In this chapter, we'll explore the strangest and most spectacular specialty museums across
America - from collections that will make you scratch your head to exhibits that will leave
you questioning reality. These are the places where ordinary objects become extraordinary
through the power of passion and preservation. Pack your sense of wonder (and perhaps
some emergency supplies) - we're about to dive into the wonderfully weird world of
America's most bizarre museums, where every visit promises not just education but the
kind of stories you'll be telling at dinner parties for years to come.

The Art of Obsession: Understanding Niche Museum Collectors and Their Motivations

In my quest to understand what drives people to create museums dedicated to items most of us would overlook, I've met collectors who can identify the manufacturing year of a vacuum cleaner by its motor hum and curators who've cataloged over 10,000 different types of barbed wire. These passionate preservationists aren't just collecting stuff - they're archiving pieces of history that somehow slipped through the cracks of mainstream museums.

At the Museum of Questionable Medical Devices[4] in Minneapolis, curator Bob McCoy once showed me his prized collection of phrenology machines while gleefully recounting how he narrowly escaped a lawsuit from a modern-day phrenology practitioner who claimed the museum's 'debunking' displays were hurting their business. "Can you believe someone's still trying to read personality traits from head bumps in the 21st century?" he chuckled, while demonstrating a particularly dubious-looking brain-measuring device from 1882.

Financial Realities of Passion Projects

The economics of maintaining these temples to the specific often reads like a chapter from a financial horror story. Take Fred's Toaster Museum[5] in Charlottesville, Virginia, which survives primarily through the sale of quirky toast-themed merchandise and an annual 'Toast-A-Thon' fundraiser where visitors compete to create art on burned bread. Fred himself supplements the museum's income by repairing vintage toasters, a skill he learned out of necessity when his collection began overwhelming his retirement savings.

From Accidental Collector to Curator

Many of these curators start their collections almost by accident. Reverend Paul Johnson, created the Pencil Sharpener Museum[6], in Logan, Ohio 20 years ago and now houses over 3,400 sharpeners, each with its own story of how it shaped American education (pun absolutely intended).

A Community of Quirky Experts

During my research, I've found that many collectors share a common origin story - they began collecting not because they were particularly interested in the objects themselves, but because they recognized these items were being lost to time.

Finding Meaning in the Mundane

The most successful niche museums have found ways to make their seemingly mundane collections relevant to modern visitors. Nancy 3, the curator of the Umbrella Cover Museum[7] in Peaks Island, Maine doesn't just display umbrella sleeves - she uses them to explore themes of loss, waste, and human forgetfulness. Each sleeve comes with a story, often funny, sometimes poignant, about how it became separated from its umbrella. "It's like a metaphor for modern life," she explained, "We're all just looking for our missing pieces."

While these collections might seem eccentric, they serve an important role in preserving aspects of American culture that larger institutions overlook. After visiting dozens of these museums, I've come to appreciate how they reflect not just their curators' obsessions, but our collective history told through the lens of everyday objects. Whether it's a collection of vintage lunch boxes that charts the evolution of popular culture or an assortment of antique fishing lures that documents changes in leisure activities, these museums piece together the story of American life one curious object at a time.

From Spam to Salami: Food-Focused Museums That Serve Up Strange History

When I first pushed open the gleaming doors of the SPAM® Museum[8] in Austin, Minnesota, the automated greeting of 'Welcome SPAMbassador!' triggered an involuntary eye roll. Two hours later, I found myself enthusiastically explaining the cultural significance of SPAM® musubi to a family from Iowa, having somehow transformed into the very SPAMbassador I'd initially mocked. That's the peculiar magic of America's food museums - they have an uncanny ability to turn skeptics into evangelists.

A Temple to Canned Meat

The SPAM® Museum itself is a 14,000-square-foot temple to Hormel's legendary canned meat, where the humble spiced ham gets the full Smithsonian treatment. Interactive exhibits trace SPAM®'s journey from World War II rations to its unexpected role as a cultural touchstone in places like Hawaii and South Korea. I watched in fascination as Betty Thomsen, a retired military cook with forty years of SPAM®-related stories, demonstrated how to make the perfect SPAM® sandwich while regaling visitors with tales of how she once had to prepare SPAM® Wellington for a visiting general who'd lost a bet.

Mustard and the Law

At the National Mustard Museum[9] in Middleton, Wisconsin, I met Barry Levenson, who left his position as an Assistant Attorney General to pursue his condiment calling. "I was wandering the supermarket aisles at 3 AM, contemplating a difficult case," he told me, "when I heard the mustards calling." What started as a middle-of-the-night epiphany has grown into a collection of over 6,090 mustards from more than 70 countries. The museum's tasting bar offers everything from classic French Dijon to a wasabi-ghost pepper blend that had me signing liability waivers. Barry proudly shared how he once successfully defended against a lawsuit from a visitor who claimed their taste buds were "permanently altered" by an particularly potent horseradish mustard – the case was dismissed when the plaintiff was caught eating spicy wings at a local bar that same evening.

Wobble Through Memory Lane

The Jell-O Gallery Museum[10] in LeRoy, New York, proves that even desserts deserve their place in history. Here, amid vintage advertisements and toy molds, I learned how a carpenter's cough remedy evolved into America's favorite wobbly dessert.

Vinegar with a Vision

But perhaps the most surprising discovery was the International Vinegar Museum[11] in Roslyn, South Dakota. Founded by Lawrence Diggs, affectionately known as "The Vinegar Man," this former high school houses what might be the world's most comprehensive collection of fermented liquids. During my visit, Diggs orchestrated a tasting that included everything from traditional balsamic to a rare pineapple vinegar that tasted like tropical sunshine with a kick. "We had a group of Italian tourists visit last summer," he chuckled, "They came to scoff but left with bottles of our homemade vinegar tucked in their luggage."

Preserving Culture, One Bite at a Time

These museums do more than preserve food history – they celebrate the unexpected ways our culinary habits shape culture. Betty Williams, a regular visitor to the Idaho Potato Museum[12] in Blackfoot, told me how she met her husband during a potato harvest tour twenty years ago. "He was trying to impress me with potato facts," she laughed, "Now we bring our grandkids here every summer." Their youngest grandson recently won the museum's annual potato-counting contest by accurately guessing the number of spuds in a massive glass jar – a feat that earned him a year's supply of potato chips and local celebrity status.

Essential Tips for the Food Museum Explorer

For the serious food museum explorer, I've learned a few essential tips:

- Avoid eating immediately before visits – most offer tastings

- Bring reading glasses for ingredient lists and historical documents

- Don't wear white clothing to anything involving condiments

- Take advantage of special events and demonstrations

- Always, always accept offers to try unusual varieties

These culinary temples might seem quirky, but they serve an essential role in preserving the stories of how food shapes our lives. Whether you're sampling exotic vinegars in South Dakota or contemplating the cultural impact of gelatin in New York, these museums remind us that every item in our pantry has a story worth preserving. Just remember to pack some antacids – enthusiasm for food history sometimes requires digestive assistance.

Interactive Oddities: Hands-On Experiences in America's Weirdest Museums

If you've ever wanted to milk a mechanical cow, pilot a salvaged UFO simulator, or experience what it's like to be digested by a giant model of the human stomach, America's hands-on museums have got you covered. I've done all three, and I can tell you that the mechanical cow was surprisingly judgmental about my technique.

A Slide Through Science

The Creation Museum[13] in Kentucky provides visitors with the opportunity to explore biblical history, breathtaking exhibitions, floral gardens, a planetarium, a zoo, a zip line adventure course, and a great deal more.

Close Encounters of the Simulated Kind

Then there's the UFO Museum[14] in Roswell, where visitors can test their alien piloting skills in a simulator cobbled together from an old flight training device and parts from a defunct arcade. The museum narrowly avoided a lawsuit when an overly enthusiastic visitor, convinced of his extraterrestrial origin, attempted an "emergency landing procedure" that resulted in the simulator nearly tipping over. Now there's a prominently displayed sign reading "Earth Natives Only Beyond This Point."

While these interactive experiences might seem gimmicky, they're often rooted in serious educational goals. The quirky presentations just make the learning more memorable. As Martha from the agricultural museum puts it, "Nobody forgets their first time being outsmarted by a mechanical cow."

Tips for Hands-On Museum Adventures

A few tips for maximizing your hands-on museum experience:

- Wear comfortable clothes you don't mind getting dirty

- Bring a change of shoes (trust me on this one)

- Don't skip the safety briefing, no matter how silly it seems

- Be prepared to sign multiple waivers

- Keep your phone in a ziplock bag

The Unexpected Experts

After weeks of wandering through America's most peculiar collections, I've gained a new appreciation for the passionate souls who dedicate their lives to preserving the weird and wonderful corners of our cultural heritage. From the banana enthusiast who rescued me from a malfunctioning spacesuit to the barbed wire expert who could identify manufacturing patterns by touch, these curators aren't just collecting objects – they're keeping amazing stories alive.

I've learned that expertise comes in the most unexpected packages. Take Susan at the Stark's Vacuum Museum[15] in Portland, who can diagnose vintage Hoovers by their sound alone and once had to testify as an expert witness in a surprisingly heated court case about historical cleaning implements.

Expect the Unexpected

These museums operate by their own mysterious rhythms – some following the curator's day job schedule, others aligned with phases of the moon or local festival calendars. Many survive on a mix of passionate volunteers, creative fundraising (the Potato Peeler Museum's annual "Speed Peeling Championship" is surprisingly competitive), and the occasional miracle. Call ahead, bring cash, and be prepared for anything. That gift shop purchase might seem bizarre now, but trust me – it'll become your favorite conversation starter.

In an age where experiences are increasingly virtual and disposable, these physical archives of the odd and obscure feel more vital than ever. They remind us that human interest knows no bounds, that one person's trash can become another's meticulously cataloged treasure, and that sometimes the most profound insights come from the most unexpected sources. Whether you're examining the world's largest collection of sock monkeys or learning about the evolution of dental floss, these museums offer windows into the beautiful specificity of human passion.

So the next time you spot a hand-painted sign advertising a collection of something you never knew existed, take that exit. Maybe you'll spend an hour examining vintage pencil sharpeners, or perhaps you'll lose an entire afternoon learning about the surprisingly dramatic history of garden gnomes. Either way, you'll walk away with stories that no algorithm could ever recommend and experiences that no virtual tour could replicate.

Just remember to pack that emergency WD-40 – you never know when you might need to escape from a vintage banana spacesuit.

Chapter 8

Food Follies

America's Weirdest Restaurants and Culinary Oddities

You Are What Surrounds You

T HEY SAY YOU ARE what you eat, but at America's weirdest restaurants, you might just be what surrounds you while you eat. From dining in complete darkness to eating in a converted prison cell, the United States has perfected the art of turning meals into theatrical productions that sometimes overshadow the food itself. From decades-old diners housed in converted train cars to restaurants where the waitstaff deliberately insults you, America's dining landscape is as diverse as it is bizarre. These establishments aren't just about filling your stomach – they're immersive experiences where each bite comes with a side of spectacle and a dash of the unexpected.

Dining as Performance

Over the years, themed restaurants have evolved far beyond the kitschy confines of rainforest cafes or medieval banquet halls. Today's culinary adventurers can dine in pitch darkness, feast in former prison cells, or watch their sushi arrive via miniature bullet train. In our Instagram-obsessed era, these venues understand that crafting a memorable atmosphere is just as crucial as perfecting their flavors.

Why We Seek Out the Strange

What drives us to seek out these gastronomic oddities? Perhaps it's our innate desire to transform mundane necessities into extraordinary adventures. Or maybe we've grown weary of cookie-cutter chain restaurants with their plastified menus and artificially enthusiastic servers. Whatever the reason, these unconventional eateries have become destinations in themselves, proving that a truly unforgettable meal requires more than just good food.

A Visit to the Heart Attack Grill

Last summer, I found myself at the Heart Attack Grill[1] in Las Vegas, where the staff dresses in nurse and doctor costumes, and customers wearing hospital gowns get wheeled to their tables. As someone who typically opts for sensible portions, I felt like an anthropologist studying a bizarre ritual as I watched a 350-pound man attempt the 'Octuple Bypass Burger' challenge. The restaurant's scales near the entrance weigh customers in front of everyone - if you're over 350 pounds, you eat free. I witnessed a gentleman celebrate this dubious achievement with both pride and a slight hint of concern. When my modest single bypass burger arrived, complete with a mandatory hospital bracelet, I couldn't help but laugh at the absurdity of it all. The waitress-nurse took my pulse dramatically before serving me, and I had to sign a waiver acknowledging the health risks of the meal. It was like dining in a carnival funhouse mirror version of a medical drama, where gluttony is celebrated and common sense goes to die. The experience taught me that sometimes the most memorable meals aren't about the food at all - they're about the story you get to tell afterward, even if that story involves explaining why you're wearing a hospital gown in your social media photos.

A Coast-to-Coast Tour of Oddball Eateries

In this chapter, we'll embark on a coast-to-coast tour of America's most outlandish eateries, from restaurants staffed by robots to establishments where dining in total darkness is the norm. We'll explore outrageous food challenges that test both stomach and sanity, uncover bizarre regional specialties, and investigate why some people willingly pay premium prices to be insulted by their servers. Consider this your passport to the wonderfully weird world of American dining – where the food might be questionable, but the memories are guaranteed to last a lifetime.

Theme Restaurants: Where Ambiance Eclipses the Menu

Picture yourself dining inside a vintage bomber plane, where the seats are ejector chairs and the menu items have names like **'Crash Landing Nachos'** and **'Turbulence Tacos.'** That's just another Tuesday night in America's ever-expanding universe of themed restaurants, where the spectacle of dining has evolved into performance art.

I once spent an evening at a ninja-themed restaurant in New York, where black-clad servers would materialize from hidden doorways to serve sushi with theatrical smoke effects. Between courses, they performed acrobatic routines that made me wonder if their culinary training included parkour certification. The food was decent, but what I remember most is nearly dropping my miso soup when a 'ninja' suddenly descended from the ceiling to refill my water glass. (Note: Don't bother looking for it since it has closed its doors forever[2]).

These theatrical eateries run the gamut from charming to downright bizarre. Take the growing trend of hospital-themed establishments, where your 'nurse' takes your order with a toy stethoscope and your burger comes with a side of surgical gloves. I visited one in Latvia where the chairs were actual wheelchairs, and the cocktails arrived via IV drip bags. The food was mediocre at best, but watching other diners struggle to maneuver their wheelchairs while balancing plates of fries was better entertainment than most Broadway shows.

The irony of these places is that as the theatrics get more elaborate, the actual cuisine often becomes an afterthought. During my quest to experience America's most outlandish dining venues, I've eaten passable pasta served by singing gondoliers in an indoor Venice, consumed lukewarm burgers in a restaurant designed to look like a maximum-security prison, and sampled surprisingly decent dim sum in a converted elementary school where servers dress as strict teachers and make you raise your hand to order.

Practical Tips for Themed Dining Adventures

For the adventurous diner, here are some practical tips I've learned the hard way:

- **Book ahead**, especially for the more popular themed venues

- **Ask about any required dress codes** or interactive elements

- **Check recent reviews** – sometimes the novelty wears off and maintenance suffers

- **Be prepared for tourist prices** – you're paying for the show as much as the sustenance

- **Bring a sense of humor** and remember that perfect cuisine isn't the point

---

Dining for the 'Gram

The psychology behind these restaurants fascinates me. In an age where we can have any cuisine delivered to our doorstep, these places understand that many diners crave more than just food – they want an experience worth sharing. It's no coincidence that the rise of themed restaurants parallels the growth of social media. After all, a photo of your standard cheeseburger might get a few likes, but a picture of you eating that same burger while seated in a coffin at a vampire-themed café? That's Instagram gold.

Flamboyant Feasts

My most memorable themed dining experience happened at The Airplane Restaurant[3], an aviation-themed restaurant in Colorado Springs. Housed in a converted Boeing 747, the establishment went all-in on the concept. The bathrooms were labeled **'First Class Lavatories,'** the bar was in the cockpit, and the waitstaff wore modified flight attendant uniforms. When I asked about vegetarian options, my server stayed perfectly in character, apologizing that **'due to unexpected turbulence, all our vegetarian meals have been rerouted to Denver.'** I ended up with a chicken sandwich that was about as flavorful as actual airplane food, but the experience of dining at 'ground level' in a jet was worth every penny.

These restaurants represent something uniquely American – our ability to take a simple concept and supersize it into spectacular entertainment. While culinary purists might scoff at places where the décor overshadows the dishes, there's an undeniable charm to establishments that prioritize fun over fine dining. They remind us that sometimes the best meals aren't about the food at all – they're about the stories we get to tell afterward.

Extreme Eating Challenges and Food Competitions

America has perfected the art of turning eating into a competitive sport, transforming ordinary restaurants into gladiatorial arenas where human determination faces off against portions that could feed a small village. I've witnessed these gastronomic battles firsthand, and let me tell you – there's nothing quite like watching someone attempt to consume their own body weight in hot wings while a crowd chants **"EAT! EAT! EAT!"**

One sweltering Saturday in Nashville, I found myself at a hot chicken challenge that would make a fire-eater flinch. The waiver I had to sign included phrases like **"temporary loss of vision"** and **"possible hallucinations."** The chicken arrived with a warning label and a pair of rubber gloves. A fellow challenger – a burly truck driver who'd boasted about his tolerance for spice – took one bite and immediately started speaking in tongues. I managed two bites before my taste buds filed for divorce and my sinuses declared independence.

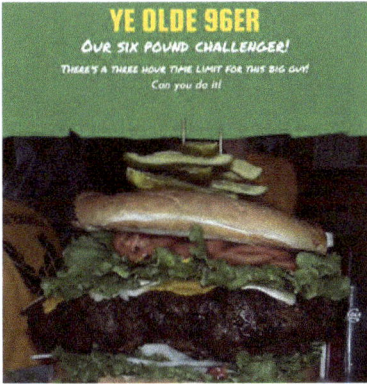

YE OLDE 96ER
OUR SIX POUND CHALLENGER!
THERE'S A THREE HOUR TIME LIMIT FOR THIS BIG GUY!
Can you do it!

These culinary competitions come in all flavors and formats. At **Denny's Beer Barrel Pub**[4] in Pennsylvania, the **'Ye Olde 96er'** challenge dares participants to devour a 6-pound burger (that's 96 ounces) complete with fixings in under 3 hours. I watched a competitive eater attempt this feat while taking detailed notes. By hour two, he had developed a thousand-yard stare that I've only seen in documentary footage of arctic expeditions.

The psychological aspect of these challenges fascinates me. It's not just about capacity – it's about strategy. Professional competitors don't just show up and start shoveling food into their faces (well, most don't). They study techniques, train their bodies, and prepare mentally. I once interviewed a competitive eater who treated hot dog eating like an Olympic sport, complete with breathing exercises and visualization techniques. He could tell you the optimal water temperature for bun-dipping with the precision of a nuclear physicist.

Tips for Aspiring Competitive Eaters

For those considering dipping their toes (or rather, their forks) into the world of competitive eating, here's what I've learned from countless hours of observation and one ill-advised attempt at a gallon-of-ice-cream challenge:

- **Research the challenge thoroughly** before attempting – success rates are usually posted online

- **Start with smaller challenges** to build your tolerance

- **Stay hydrated**, but don't fill up on liquids

- **Pace yourself** – most people crash in the first ten minutes

- **Accept that dignity is not part of the equation**

The phenomenon has evolved far beyond county fair pie-eating contests. Social media has transformed these gut-busting endeavors into viral spectacles, with restaurants constantly pushing the boundaries of what constitutes a **"reasonable"** portion size. I've seen everything from yard-long sushi rolls to pizzas that require a building permit.

But perhaps the most memorable challenge I witnessed wasn't about size at all. It was a tiny diner in Texas with a deceptively simple challenge: finish three tacos in fifteen minutes. The catch? They contained a sauce made from **Carolina Reaper peppers** that registered high enough on the Scoville scale to qualify as a weapon in some states. The prize was just $50, but the real reward was bragging rights and a photo on the **'Wall of Flame.'** I watched competitor after competitor approach with confidence and leave with a new appreciation for dairy products (milk being the only thing that brought relief).

These gastronomic gauntlets represent something uniquely American – our ability to turn anything, even eating, into a competitive sport worthy of spectators and statistics. They're ridiculous, potentially dangerous, and completely fascinating. Just remember that while watching these events can be entertaining, participating requires careful consideration and possibly a good health insurance plan.

As for me? I've learned to appreciate these challenges from a safe distance, usually with a sensibly portioned meal in front of me. After all, someone needs to document these feats of culinary courage, and it's hard to take notes when you're trying to finish a burger the size of a steering wheel.

Unusual Food Combinations and Regional Oddities

Deep in the heart of Minnesota, I once watched in fascination as a local diner served what they proudly called a **'grape salad'** – a concoction that contained neither salad nor fresh grapes, but rather a mystifying combination of sour cream, cream cheese, and sugar-coated grapes that had clearly never met a vegetable. This, I learned, was just the tip of the culinary oddity iceberg in America's heartland.

The landscape of American regional food quirks reads like a mad scientist's cookbook. In **St. Louis**, they take perfectly good pizza and transform it into something entirely different using **Provel** – a processed cheese product that's essentially the result of provolone, Swiss, and cheddar cheese having an identity crisis. The first time I tried it, I spent ten minutes trying to decide if I loved it or if my taste buds were simply too confused to form an opinion.

During a road trip through **Cincinnati**, I found myself face-to-face with their infamous chili – a Mediterranean-spiced meat sauce served over spaghetti and topped with a mountain of finely shredded cheddar cheese. The locals have developed an entire ordering language around it:

- **Three-way** (spaghetti, chili, cheese)

- **Four-way** (add onions or beans)

- **Five-way** (the whole shebang)

My first bite was a revelation – not because it was necessarily good or bad, but because it completely redefined my understanding of what constitutes chili.

The **South** deserves special recognition in any discussion of unusual food combinations. At a gas station in rural **Georgia**, I discovered **peanuts in Coca-Cola** – a tradition that involves dumping salted peanuts directly into a bottle of Coke. The elderly gentleman who introduced me to this combination watched with obvious delight as I tried to figure out the logistics of drinking while avoiding a peanut avalanche. **"The trick,"** he advised, **"is to commit to the experience."**

In **Utah**, I encountered **fry sauce** – a seemingly simple blend of ketchup and mayonnaise that locals defend with the passion usually reserved for family recipes passed down through generations. Ask about its origins, and you'll likely spark a debate that could last longer than your meal. One diner owner spent thirty minutes explaining to me why his ratio of ketchup to mayonnaise was mathematically perfect, complete with hand-drawn diagrams on a napkin.

The **Pacific Northwest** contributes its own chapter to this story with the **geoduck** (pronounced *'gooey-duck'*) – a giant clam that looks like something from a sci-fi movie. My first encounter with this regional delicacy involved a lot of nervous laughter and several attempts at photos that wouldn't get flagged as inappropriate on social media. The taste was surprisingly mild, but I'll never forget the look on my server's face when I asked if they could make it into a sandwich.

Some regional specialties seem designed specifically to test the limits of human curiosity. In **Michigan's Upper Peninsula**, the **pasty** (pronounced *'pass-tee'*) reigns supreme – a hand pie filled with meat, potatoes, and rutabaga that miners carried for lunch. When I asked a local if they ever updated the recipe, you'd think I'd suggested rewriting their constitution. **"Why mess with perfection?"** she asked, before launching into a passionate defense of rutabaga's crucial role in proper pasty construction.

Alaska offers up **Eskimo Ice Cream (Akutaq)**, traditionally made with whipped fat and berries. The modern versions I tried used Crisco instead of the traditional animal fat, but still maintained a unique texture that prompted me to reconsider everything I thought I knew about dessert. The woman who served it to me explained how her grandmother used to make it with seal oil, adding, **"This version is for tourists – we're easing you in gently."**

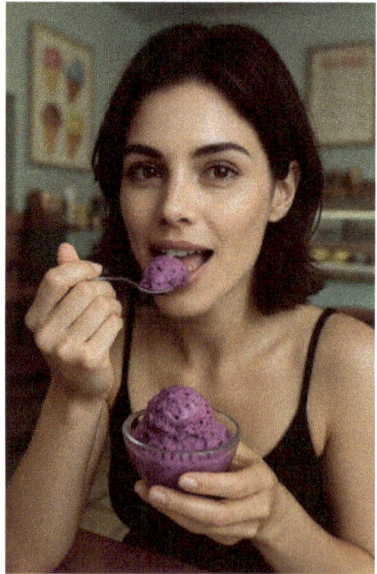

What fascinates me most about these regional oddities is how fiercely locals defend them. Suggest to someone from Indiana that their fried brain sandwich might be unusual, and you'll quickly find yourself in a spirited discussion about culinary heritage and tradition. These dishes aren't just food – they're **edible artifacts of local history, culture, and identity.**

The First Bite Philosophy

Just remember: approaching regional specialties requires an open mind and a flexible palate. What seems bizarre to outsiders is often a beloved comfort food to locals. I've learned to adopt what I call the **'first bite philosophy'** – reserve judgment until after you've actually tried something. After all, today's culinary oddity might become tomorrow's favorite food memory, even if that memory involves figuring out how to drink a Coke full of peanuts without choking.

As I sit here writing this conclusion, nursing a mild case of heartburn from my latest culinary adventure (**a five-alarm chili served by a robot in a cowboy hat**), I can't help but marvel at America's wonderfully weird relationship with food. From hospital-themed burger joints to underground supper clubs in abandoned subway stations, we've elevated the simple act of eating into performance art, competitive sport, and cultural statement all rolled into one deep-fried package.

These establishments aren't just about shock value or Instagram opportunities – though there's certainly plenty of both. They're living testaments to American ingenuity, entrepreneurial spirit, and our endless capacity to find joy in the absurd. Each themed restaurant, extreme eating challenge, and bizarre regional specialty tells a story about the people and places that created it.

I've learned that the best dining experiences often have little to do with Michelin stars or celebrity chefs. Sometimes they're found in converted train cars where the waitstaff deliberately insults you, or in tiny diners where the local specialty involves combining ingredients that should never meet. These places remind us that **food isn't just fuel** – it's an adventure, a social experiment, and occasionally, a chance to sign a medical waiver before your appetizer arrives.

So the next time you're planning a road trip or exploring a new city, consider skipping the chain restaurants and seeking out these temples of culinary weirdness. Order the mysterious regional specialty that makes outsiders scratch their heads. Accept the challenge to eat something larger than your torso. Let yourself be served by ninjas or dine in complete darkness. Your taste buds might question your judgment, but I guarantee you'll come away with stories worth sharing.

Just remember to bring an open mind, a sense of humor, and possibly some antacids. Because in America's weird and wonderful food scene, **dinner isn't just a meal – it's an experience waiting to become a story.** And sometimes, that story involves explaining to your friends back home why you have a certificate of completion from a restaurant hanging on your wall, right next to a photo of you in a hospital gown, triumphantly holding a burger the size of a hubcap.

Chapter 9

Ghost Towns and Oddball Architecture

Strange Structures and Their Stories

A S I GAZED UP at the **Winchester Mystery House**[1] in San Jose, California, I couldn't help but wonder if Sarah Winchester's architects had been taking design cues from an M.C. Escher drawing while under the influence of strong hallucinogens. The 160-room mansion, with its stairs that lead to nowhere and doors that open into solid walls, stands as testament to humanity's capacity to create architectural chaos when armed with unlimited funds and questionable judgment. These architectural curiosities scattered across America represent more than just eccentric buildings – they're **physical manifestations of dreams, obsessions, and sometimes pure madness.**

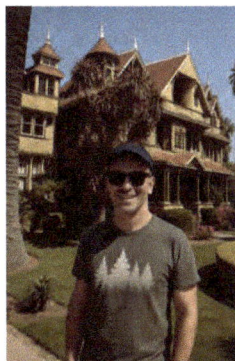

From the recycled realm of **Solomon's Castle**[2] in Florida, built entirely from discarded materials and aluminum printing plates, to other equally bizarre and brilliant monuments to the imagination, these structures prove that one person's architectural fever dream can become another's bucket list destination.

In my quest to document America's strangest buildings, I've crawled through **bottle houses in Nevada**, marveled at **folk art castles in Tennessee**, and gotten thoroughly lost in structures where basic geometry seems more like a polite suggestion than a rule. These aren't your typical tourist attractions – they're **testaments to human**

creativity, eccentricity, and our endless capacity to build things that make others scratch their heads and ask, *'What were they thinking?'*

Even our **ghost towns** tell stories that go beyond their empty streets and weathered buildings. Places like **Bodie, California**[3], preserved in a state of *'arrested decay,'* or the **underground passages beneath Seattle's Pioneer Square**[4], reveal layers of history frozen in time. These abandoned places aren't just empty buildings – they're **time capsules waiting to be discovered** by anyone brave enough to venture off the beaten path.

During my visit to **Centralia, Pennsylvania**[5] – America's infamous ghost town that's been burning underground since 1962 – I learned an important lesson about following GPS directions blindly. My trusty navigation app, apparently unaware that most of the town's roads had been reclaimed by nature, confidently directed me to 'turn left' onto what was now a crack in the earth venting steam. As I stood there, watching wisps of smoke curl up from the ground while my phone insisted I drive through what was essentially a **portal to the underworld**, I couldn't help but laugh at the absurdity of the situation. I parked my car and decided to explore on foot instead, keeping a safe distance from the various fissures and subsidence zones.

The **abandoned houses and buckled streets** told a story more compelling than any horror movie – a real-life tale of how an underground mine fire transformed a thriving coal town into a modern-day ghost town. As I photographed the cracked highways and steam vents, a local resident (one of the few who refused to leave) approached to share stories about the town's history. He pointed out places where thermometers stuck in the ground would melt and explained how residents used to check their basement temperatures daily before the evacuation. That day taught me that sometimes the most memorable travel experiences come from **ignoring your GPS and embracing the eerie beauty of America's forgotten places.**

In this chapter, we'll explore these architectural oddities and ghost towns, uncovering the strange stories behind their creation and abandonment. Pack your flashlight and wear sturdy shoes – we're about to venture into places where conventional architecture takes a backseat to imagination and where forgotten stories wait around every crooked corner.

America's Most Intriguing Ghost Towns: From Bodie to Bannack

I first visited **Bodie** on a crisp autumn morning when the Sierra Nevada air felt sharp enough to slice through my jacket. The California State Park's famous *'arrested decay'* policy has frozen this gold-mining boomtown in a **perpetual twilight between existence and oblivion** – much like my apartment during finals week back in college. As I peered through dusty windows at tables still set for dinner that was abandoned nearly a century ago, I couldn't shake the feeling that the town's 10,000 former residents had simply stepped out for a moment and forgotten to return.

Walking Bodie's weathered boardwalks, I encountered the **ghost of the American Dream in its purest form.** The **Methodist Church**[6] stands resolute against the wind, its spire reaching skyward like a finger pointing to heaven – or perhaps accusing it. Inside Bodie's saloons, **bottles still line shelves** where miners once drowned their sorrows in whiskey that probably tasted like liquid regret. A **pool table sits waiting for players** who left mid-game, probably heading to the bar for *'just one more round'* sometime around 1932.

I discovered why Bodie deserves its reputation for being one of America's best-preserved ghost towns – not because it's pristine (it isn't), but because it **feels genuinely abandoned rather than curated** for tourists. That might have something to do with the last few miles of **teeth-rattling dirt road** you have to navigate to reach it.

Pro tip: if you're renting a car, spring for the extra insurance. Your suspension will thank you later.

Up in **Montana, Bannack**[7] offers a different flavor of abandonment altogether. As the state's **first territorial capital**, it managed to maintain slightly more dignity than Bodie's notorious reputation for lawlessness – though that's not saying much considering Bannack's **sheriff turned out to be the leader of a ruthless road agent gang.** The kind of career pivot that probably wouldn't look great on LinkedIn.

The **Bannack schoolhouse** stands as a poignant reminder of frontier optimism, its **empty desks facing forward** as if still waiting for lessons to resume. The **Hotel Meade**, once the grandest building in town, now hosts only **dust motes that dance in sunbeams** streaming through broken windows. I spent an afternoon photographing its elegant staircase, wondering how many hopeful miners had climbed those steps dreaming of striking it rich.

Tips for Visiting Ghost Towns

Both towns share some common wisdom for visitors:

- **Wear sturdy shoes** – these aren't places where flip-flops are appropriate unless you're trying to become a permanent resident

- **Timing is everything** – visit during shoulder seasons when the weather is mild and you won't have to share the ghost town with too many living people

- **Avoid extremes** – summer brings intense heat and crowds, while winter can make access challenging

---

Nothing ruins the spooky atmosphere quite like getting your car stuck in a snowbank.

More importantly, these places deserve our respect. They're not just Instagram backgrounds or movie sets – they're time capsules of American ambition and failure. As I watched the sun set behind Bodie's mill, casting long shadows across the sage-covered hills, I thought about how quickly fortunes can change. One day you're living in a bustling boomtown, the next you're leaving your dinner dishes on the table and never coming back.

A Note on Souvenirs

A quick word about souvenirs: **don't take them.** Not just because it's illegal (it is) or because park rangers bring worse luck than any ghost could (they do), but because these places **need to remain intact for future generations** to explore.

Besides, according to local legend, anything taken from Bodie carries a curse. Having accidentally tracked some Bodie dirt home in my boots once and subsequently experienced a month of suspiciously bad luck, **I'm not inclined to test that theory further.**

These ghost towns serve as **powerful reminders that every boom eventually faces its bust**, every gold rush its last nugget. They're preserved now not just as tourist attractions, but as **lessons in impermanence and the fickle nature of fortune.** Walking their empty streets, you can't help but wonder what future generations will make of our own abandoned places – though hopefully, our modern ghost towns will have better cell service.

DIY Castles and Passion Projects: Solo-Built Architectural Wonders

Nothing quite captures the American spirit of **architectural rebellion** like someone who wakes up one morning and decides to build a castle with their bare hands. These **passion projects** often blur the line between architecture and obsession. In **Forestville, California**, the late **John Guidotti** spent decades transforming his property into '**The Guidotti Castle**[8],' complete with a moat, drawbridge, and enough stonework to make a quarry jealous. When I visited, I met his daughter, who continues to maintain the property. *"Dad never drew up plans,"* she told me. *"He just started building and didn't stop until physics made him."*

What strikes me about these solo-built wonders isn't just their impressive scale or unique design choices – it's the **pure, unfiltered vision behind them**. These aren't buildings designed by committee or shaped by focus groups. They're **raw expressions of individual creativity**, unburdened by practical considerations like *'building codes'* or *'structural engineering principles.'*

The beauty of these structures lies in their **imperfection**. Every crooked stone, every slightly off-kilter window, tells the story of someone who **refused to let their lack of formal training stand in the way of their architectural dreams**. They remind us that sometimes the most impressive achievements come not from careful planning, but from the simple act of **starting something and refusing to stop**.

Visiting Tips

When visiting these DIY monuments:

- Bring **sturdy shoes**

- Expect uneven terrain and **unconventional staircases**

- Tours are often guided by the **builder themselves**

That's exactly what makes these places special – they're not just buildings, they're **autobiographies written in stone, metal, and occasional beer cans.**

For those inspired to follow in these builders' footsteps, perhaps **start smaller**. While building your own full-scale castle might be a bit ambitious for a weekend project, the DIY castle-building spirit can be channeled into more manageable forms. After all, every great solo-built wonder started with someone looking at a pile of materials and thinking, *'I could make something amazing with this.'*

These passion projects stand as **monuments to individual vision and perseverance** in the American landscape. They remind us that sometimes the most interesting destinations aren't created by committees or corporations, but by **single individuals** who wake up one day and decide, *'You know what? I think I'll build a castle.'* Each crooked stone and welded joint tells a story of determination, creativity, and perhaps a healthy dose of **productive stubbornness**.

Roadside Architectural Oddities: Houses Built from Bottles, Newspapers, and Other Unusual Materials

In a world obsessed with **sleek minimalism** and smart homes, there's something wonderfully defiant about a house built from **empty beer bottles**. I discovered this truth while standing before the **Rhyolite Bottle House**[9] in Nevada, watching sunlight dance through walls made from **50,000 glass vessels**. The kaleidoscopic display reminded me of a stained glass window designed by someone who'd spent a bit too much time at the saloon.

Tom Kelly, the house's original builder, didn't set out to create an artistic masterpiece in 1906. He was just a pragmatic 76-year-old miner facing a lumber shortage in the middle of the desert. Looking at the growing collection of empty bottles around the mining camp, he saw what most of us would miss – **load-bearing walls waiting to happen**. The result is a structure that turns the desert sun into an ever-changing light show, though I imagine the morning after a night of drinking might have been particularly challenging for the original residents.

During my visit, I met a local photographer who'd been documenting the bottle house for years. *"Every season, every hour brings different colors,"* she told me, adjusting her camera settings. *"It's like the house is alive."* She wasn't wrong. As clouds passed overhead, the walls shifted from emerald to amber, creating patterns that would make a kaleidoscope jealous.

Though I couldn't help but wonder about the **structural integrity of walls made from containers designed to hold liquid courage**, the house has survived over a century of desert winds and curious tourists.

In **Simi Valley, California**, I encountered another monument to architectural recycling – **Grandma Prisbrey's Bottle Village**[10]. **Tressa 'Grandma' Prisbrey** started building her glass wonderland in 1956, at age 60, crafting **seventeen structures from over a million bottles** and various discarded treasures. She claimed she began building simply because she needed a place to store her **pencil collection** – all **17,000** of them. Sometimes the most extraordinary projects start with the most ordinary needs.

The paths through Bottle Village wind past walls composed of everything from **champagne bottles to old television sets**. Every turn reveals another surprise: a **dolls-head birdbath** here, a **wall of blue milk of magnesia bottles** there. It's like walking through someone's memories, if those memories had been sorted by color and cemented together.

One common thread connects these unusual structures – they're all products of **necessity meeting creativity**, with a healthy dose of **'why not?'** thrown in. Their builders saw possibilities in materials others had discarded, **turning trash into architectural treasures**.

Visiting Tips

- Visit **bottle houses** during early morning or late afternoon for the most dramatic light

- Bring a **camera with manual settings** – the interplay of light and glass can be tricky

- Most importantly, **bring an open mind**

These aren't just buildings; they're **works of art that double as shelter**, proof that one person's trash can become another's architectural legacy.

The **preservation** of these unique structures presents its own challenges. **Weather, time, and the occasional earthquake** threaten their survival. Yet **dedicated preservationists** work to maintain these pieces of American architectural history, understanding that they represent more than just unusual building techniques – they're **physical reminders of human creativity and resourcefulness**.

As I stood in the cool shade of the Rhyolite Bottle House one last time, watching shadows play across the glass-studded walls, I thought about how these structures represent the best kind of recycling – **the kind that transforms the ordinary into the extraordinary**.

Reflections on America's Architectural Oddities

Amid the crumbling walls and crooked towers of America's architectural oddities, I've discovered that the most fascinating structures often arise from the most improbable dreams. From **Winchester's endless staircases** to **Bishop's hand-built castle**, these places remind us that **architecture isn't just about following blueprints** – sometimes it's about following your peculiar vision wherever it leads, even if that means building a house from 50,000 empty bottles.

Exploring these unconventional buildings and ghost towns has taught me that **beauty doesn't always wear a familiar face**. Sometimes it shows up in the form of a castle welded together by one determined man, or in the haunting silence of a town where the streets have literally caught fire. These places might not make it into architectural textbooks, but they tell stories **far more interesting than any perfectly planned subdivision ever could.**

As development continues to **standardize our built environment**, these **architectural rebels** become increasingly precious. They stand as **monuments to individual vision**, to the American spirit of *"why not?"*, and to the simple truth that sometimes the best places to visit are the ones that **make absolutely no sense on paper.**

In the end, these architectural oddities and abandoned places offer more than just unusual photo opportunities or interesting stories to share. They remind us that in a world increasingly dominated by algorithms and efficiency, there's still room for the **wonderfully weird, the impractical, and the purely passionate**.

They suggest that maybe the best kind of architecture isn't about perfection at all – it's about having the **courage to build something uniquely your own**, even if everyone else thinks you've lost your mind.

So the next time you're driving down a dusty back road and spot a glinting tower made of **hubcaps** or a house that seems to defy several laws of physics, **take that detour**. After all, in a country where one person's trash regularly becomes another person's **load-bearing wall**, you never know what architectural wonders await around the next bend.
Just watch out for those steam vents in Centralia – some architectural features are best admired from a safe distance.

Chapter 10

Festivals of the Freaky

Celebrating America's Strangest Traditions

W HILE MOST TOURISTS FLOCK to Times Square for New Year's Eve or crowd onto the National Mall for Fourth of July fireworks, there exists a parallel universe of American celebrations that are decidedly more peculiar. In small towns and city streets across the country, locals gather to chuck frozen dead fish over state lines, race outhouses through snow-covered streets, and celebrate everything from roadkill to extraterrestrial visitors. From Earlville, Iowa's celebration of leftover Christmas fruitcake to Manitou Springs, Colorado's annual Emma Crawford Coffin Races[1], there's something delightfully eccentric about how small towns turn their local quirks into full-blown festivals. These celebrations serve as a reminder that sometimes the best entertainment doesn't come with a hefty price tag or a corporate sponsor – just a healthy dose of community spirit and an appreciation for the absurd.

What makes these festivals truly special isn't just their peculiar premises, but the passionate locals who pour their hearts into transforming mundane objects and obscure historical events into spectacular celebrations. Take the International Cherry Pit Spitting Championship[2] in Eau Claire, Michigan, where competitors train year-round to launch cherry pits with the dedication of Olympic athletes. Or consider the Frozen Dead Guy Days[3] in Nederland, Colorado, which celebrates a cryogenically frozen Norwegian grandfather with coffin races, frozen t-shirt contests, and appropriately morbid merriment.

These festivals represent more than just quirky entertainment – they're living time capsules of local history, economic lifelines for small communities, and gathering places where strangers become friends over shared absurdity. In Rollag, Minnesota, the Western Minnesota Steam Threshers Reunion[4] transforms a quiet prairie town into a steam-powered wonderland, where enthusiasts maintain century-old machines with religious devotion. Meanwhile, the Gilroy Garlic Festival [5]in California proves that even the humblest bulb can become a cultural touchstone, drawing tens of thousands of visitors and generating crucial revenue for local businesses.

In this chapter, we'll explore these wonderfully weird celebrations, complete with practical tips on:

- Timing your visits

- Finding affordable accommodations during festival peaks

- Fully immersing yourself in local traditions without looking like a complete tourist (or at least how to embrace looking like one with dignity)

You'll learn:

- Which festivals are family-friendly

- Which ones require advance planning

- And most importantly, which ones have the best food – because let's face it, half the reason we attend these events is to try deep-fried whatever-they're-serving-this-year

So pack your sense of adventure, leave your inhibitions at home, and prepare to discover a side of America where community spirit thrives in the most unexpected ways. Whether you're watching teams race beds through downtown streets or joining a massive pillow fight in the town square, these festivals remind us that sometimes the most memorable travel experiences are the ones that make the least sense on paper but the most sense in your heart.

Food Fight Festivities: From Garlic to Spam

I discovered the true meaning of 'food festival' at my first Gilroy Garlic Festival when I accidentally wandered into the cooking demonstration area just as a chef was attempting to set a world record for most cloves peeled in one minute. The air was thick with allium-induced tears, and somewhere in the crowd, someone was definitely regretting their garlic ice cream decision. But that's the beauty of America's food-centric celebrations – they transform ordinary ingredients into extraordinary spectacles.

The Gilroy Garlic Festival

The Gilroy Garlic Festival isn't just about making vampires nervous; it's a testament to how a small agricultural community turned their pungent crop into an economic powerhouse. Watching amateur chefs compete in the Great Garlic Cook-off, I witnessed creativity that bordered on culinary madness. One contestant's garlic-infused birthday cake might not have won any prizes, but it certainly won the award for 'Most Likely to Keep Your Date at Arm's Length.' The festival generates over $10 million annually for local nonprofits, proving that sometimes the best way to help your community is to embrace your stinkiest assets.

🧄 Gilroy Garlic Festival – Tourist Fact Sheet

Category	Details
Name	Gilroy Garlic Festival
Location	Gilroy, California – proudly the "Garlic Capital of the World"
Type of Event	Annual community food & culture festival celebrating all things garlic
First Held	1979
Usual Timing	Late July (varies; recent years feature smaller pop-up events)
Signature Experiences	🏆 Great Garlic Cook-Off 🧄 Gourmet Alley food court 🎵 Live music & entertainment 🎀 Garlic braiding demos
Cuisine Highlights	Garlic fries, garlic ice cream, garlic-stuffed mushrooms, and experimental creations like garlic birthday cake
Attendance	Historically up to 100,000 visitors per event
Community Impact	Over $10 million raised for local nonprofits and charities
Accessibility	Outdoor venue with accessible facilities and shuttle options
Parking	Typically supported by off-site lots and shuttle service
Recent Changes	Large-scale festival paused; now organized as pop-up events and fundraisers via the Gilroy Garlic Festival Association
Website	gilroygarlicfestivalassociation.com
Fun Fact	In one year's cook-off, a garlic birthday cake stole the show—not for taste, but for its breath-clearing superpowers.

Waikiki's Spam Jam

Over in Waikiki, the annual Spam Jam[6] transforms Kalakaua Avenue into a celebration of the canned meat that somehow became Hawaii's unofficial state food. During my visit, I found myself in a heated debate with a local chef about the correct pronunciation of 'musubi' while sampling Spam cheesecake – a combination that shouldn't work but somehow does. The festival isn't just about questionable culinary experiments; it's a reminder of how World War II transformed local food culture, with Spam becoming a sought-after commodity during rationing. Today, Hawaii consumes more Spam per capita than any other state, and the festival has become a crucial driver of tourism during the spring shoulder season.

Waikiki Spam Jam – Tourist Fact Sheet

Category	Details
Name	Waikiki Spam Jam Festival
Location	Kalakaua Avenue, Waikiki, Honolulu, Oʻahu, Hawaiʻi
Type of Event	Annual street festival celebrating Hawaiʻi's love affair with Spam
First Held	2003
Usual Timing	Late April or early May (Spring shoulder season)
Signature Experiences	Spam Musubi tastings Spam-themed desserts (yes, cheesecake!) Hawaiian music & hula performances Local arts, crafts & vendor booths
Food Culture Fun Fact	Hawaiʻi consumes more Spam per capita than any other U.S. state
Historical Roots	Spam became widely consumed in WWII due to military rations and supply shortages
Street Closure	Kalakaua Avenue is closed for the event; becomes a pedestrian-only festival zone
Community Impact	Supports the Hawaiʻi Foodbank and local nonprofits
Accessibility	Wheelchair and stroller-friendly with public transit access nearby
Website	spamjamhawaii.com
Fun Fact	One year featured **Spam cheesecake**—and yes, it was oddly delicious. Bonus points if you pronounce "musubi" correctly under pressure.

Tomato Fights and Fruitcake Flight

For those seeking actual food fights, several American cities have attempted to recreate Spain's La Tomatina, though with considerably more insurance waivers and safety goggles. At the Midwest Tomato Fest[7] in Columbia Station, Ohio, I learned that white clothing is both the best and worst choice for a tomato fight – terrible for stains but excellent for dramatic battle photos. The event uses overripe tomatoes that would otherwise go to waste, combining messy fun with food waste reduction. Those signature white t-shirts? They're biodegradable and made from recycled materials.

🍅 Tomato Fights – Tourist Fact Sheet

Category	Details
Name	Midwest Tomato Fest (and similar U.S. tomato fight events)
Notable Location	Columbia Station, Ohio (among others across the U.S.)
Inspired By	Spain's La Tomatina – but with more waivers, safety goggles, and OSHA vibes
Main Features	🍅 Massive tomato fight with overripe, unsellable tomatoes 👕 White biodegradable t-shirts provided 🎵 DJs, live music, beer gardens, and "pre-splat" warm-ups
Timing	Typically held in summer months (dates vary)
Eco Focus	All tomatoes used are past-edible and would otherwise be discarded
Attire Tip	White shirts = better photos, worse laundry odds
Safety Measures	Eye protection encouraged; tomatoes must be squished before throwing
Community Angle	Often raises money for local food banks or farm sustainability orgs
Fun Fact	The shirts may stain permanently... but at least they biodegrade with dignity.

Great Fruitcake Toss

My personal favorite remains Manitou Springs' Great Fruitcake Toss[8], where holiday regifting reaches Olympic proportions. After watching a team of engineers launch a fruitcake 125 feet using a medieval-style trebuchet, I asked the obvious question: "Why fruitcake?" The answer from a local organizer was simple: "Because nobody actually wants to eat them." The event has evolved into an engineering challenge that brings together food waste awareness, physics education, and the universal desire to see desserts achieve flight.

⚙ Great Fruitcake Toss – Tourist Fact Sheet

Category	Details
Name	Great Fruitcake Toss
Location	Manitou Springs, Colorado
Type of Event	Holiday-Themed Food Fling / Engineering Competition
First Held	1996
Timing	Typically early January (after the holidays, naturally)
Main Attractions	⚙ Fruitcake launching via hand, slingshot, catapult, and trebuchet ⚙ Engineering team challenges ⚙ Physics education meets pastry demolition
Why Fruitcake?	Because nobody wants to eat them. Also: they're dense, durable, and aerodynamic(ish).
Community Impact	Promotes food waste awareness and creative reuse
Competitions	Distance toss, team launches, creative costumes, and absurd delivery devices
Accessibility	Outdoor park setting; all ages welcome
Fun Fact	One team launched a fruitcake **125 feet** using a medieval-style **trebuchet** — because science. And spite.

Festival Survival Guide

Before attending any food festival, particularly those involving airborne edibles, remember the cardinal rules:

- Wear clothes you're willing to sacrifice to the food gods

- Bring a waterproof camera case

- Never, under any circumstances, forget to pack antacids

Most importantly, check festival websites well in advance – many require:

- Pre-registration

- Specific rules about participation

For example, the Tomato Fest requires signing a waiver acknowledging that yes, you're voluntarily choosing to be pelted with produce.

These festivals do more than just celebrate food – they:

- Create economic opportunities for small towns

- Preserve cultural traditions

- Prove that Americans will absolutely turn anything into a competition

They remind us that sometimes the best travel experiences involve:

- Embracing the absurd

- Trying the questionable

- Accepting that yes, maybe Spam ice cream is worth trying once in your life

Just maybe not right before boarding a crowded airplane.

Weather-Predicting Animals and Their Annual Ceremonies

If you've ever wondered why we entrust our seasonal forecasts to drowsy rodents in top hats, blame the Germans. Not the modern ones – we're talking about the Pennsylvania Dutch settlers who brought their weather-predicting traditions to America, swapping European badgers for the more readily available groundhog. I discovered this historical tidbit while shivering in the pre-dawn darkness at Gobbler's Knob, watching men in top hats and tails ceremoniously consult with a slightly confused groundhog named Phil.

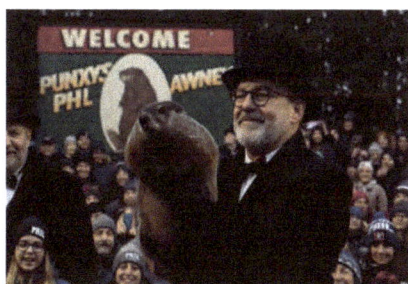

The annual Groundhog Day[9] celebration in Punxsutawney isn't just about meteorological marmots – it's an economic engine that transforms a quiet town of 5,500 into a tourist hub hosting 30,000 visitors each February. Local hotels book solid months in advance, restaurants serve groundhog-themed specials (though thankfully not made from actual groundhogs), and gift shops do their best business of the year selling everything from Phil plushies to forecast-themed fortune cookies.

But Phil isn't the only animal meteorologist on America's payroll. Down in Texas, I witnessed the annual emergence of Bee Cave Bob[10], where an armadillo's Groundhog Day counterpart predictions come with a distinctly Texan twist. The ceremony involves the 'Benevolent Knights of the Raccoon' – a group whose official uniforms include cowboy hats and pressed Western shirts – interpreting Bob's behavior for a crowd of early-rising enthusiasts. Unlike his Pennsylvania cousin, Bob doesn't just predict weather; he's also expected to forecast the state's political climate, though his accuracy rate on both fronts remains suspiciously unaudited.

In New Iberia, Louisiana, Pierre C. Shadeaux[11], a nutria (essentially a swamp rat with better PR), draws crowds to predict not winter's length but the severity of the upcoming hurricane season. The irony of using an invasive species to predict natural disasters isn't lost on locals, who've masterfully transformed an environmental pest into a beloved mascot. During my visit, I watched as city officials treated this oversized rodent with the gravitas typically reserved for visiting dignitaries, while local schoolchildren performed a surprisingly catchy song about wetland conservation.

These ceremonies have evolved far beyond simple weather prediction into full-blown cultural phenomena. Take General Beauregard Lee[12], Georgia's prognosticating ground-hog, who holds honorary doctorates from the University of Georgia and Georgia State University – making him arguably more qualified than some human meteorologists. His annual ceremony at the Yellow River Game Ranch includes a breakfast of hash browns from Waffle House, proving that even weather-predicting rodents appreciate scattered, smothered, and covered.

The economic impact of these events extends beyond tourist dollars. Many communities use their animal oracles as focal points for broader winter festivals, creating much-needed revenue during otherwise slow seasons. Punxsutawney's Groundhog Day celebration, for instance, has spawned an entire week of events including art shows, chainsaw carving demonstrations, and the 'Phil Phest' music festival – because nothing says 'winter weather prediction' quite like live bands playing in hypothermia-inducing temperatures.

Attending one of these ceremonies requires careful planning and a high tolerance for early mornings. Most predictions happen at dawn, presumably because these animals are early risers or, more likely, because someone decided that if they had to be up that early, everyone else should suffer too. Pack accordingly: warm clothes, comfortable shoes, and enough caffeine to make standing in freezing temperatures while awaiting a rodent's weather report seem perfectly reasonable.

For the best experience, arrive the day before and immerse yourself in the pre-prediction festivities. Many towns host evening celebrations where you can mingle with locals and learn the surprisingly complex lore surrounding their animal oracles. In Punxsutawney, the 'Groundhog Club' inner circle members share stories of Phil's supposedly eternal life (maintained through sips of magical 'groundhog punch') with the same solemnity as medieval historians discussing royal lineages.

These celebrations remind us that sometimes the most enduring traditions aren't about accuracy or logic – they're about communities coming together to embrace their unique identity, even if that identity involves dressing up in Victorian-era clothing to consult with a groundhog. They're about finding joy in the depths of winter, creating economic opportunities from unlikely sources, and maintaining cultural traditions that connect us to our quirky past.

Just remember, whether you're watching a groundhog in Pennsylvania, an armadillo in Texas, or a nutria in Louisiana, these ceremonies are less about accurate meteorology and more about celebrating the wonderful absurdity of human nature. After all, any tradition that involves consulting sleepy animals about seasonal changes while wearing formal attire is clearly more focused on the journey than the destination.

Extraterrestrial Celebrations and UFO Festivals

In my never-ending quest to document America's quirkiest gatherings, I've found myself in more than a few UFO festivals where the line between fact and fantasy becomes delightfully blurred. These celebrations transform sleepy towns into cosmic carnivals where tinfoil hats are considered haute couture and green face paint is practically black-tie attire.

Roswell, New Mexico

Take Roswell's UFO Festival, the mothership of all extraterrestrial celebrations. Each July, this New Mexico town of 48,000 swells to over 100,000 visitors, all seeking their own close encounters of the festive kind. During my last visit, I watched as downtown transformed into an interplanetary block party where retired Air Force personnel shared panel space with self-proclaimed alien abductees, and local grandmothers sold alien-shaped cookies alongside UFO researchers hawking their latest books.

The festival's economic impact is anything but theoretical – hotels book solid months in advance, restaurants serve galaxy-themed specials, and even the most skeptical shop owners find themselves stocking alien merchandise. One local diner owner told me his 'Area 51 Burger' (complete with green chile sauce and mysterious glowing sauce) outsells every other menu item three-to-one during festival week, proving that extraterrestrial tourism can indeed put Earth dollars in earthling pockets.

🛸 Roswell UFO Festival – Tourist Fact Sheet

Category	Details
Name	Roswell UFO Festival
Location	Roswell, New Mexico
Type of Event	Sci-Fi / Pop Culture Festival with Historical and Conspiracy Themes
First Held	1995 (to mark the 1947 "Roswell Incident" anniversary)
Timing	Every July, typically around the 4th weekend
Attendance	Town of 48,000 swells to over **100,000 visitors** during peak weekends
Signature Experiences	👽 Alien costume contests 🛸 Panels with ufologists, authors, and eyewitnesses ➤ Alien-themed art, food, parades & cosplay 🍪 Alien cookies and crafts by locals
Key Locations	Roswell Convention Center, International UFO Museum, Main Street district
Community Blend	Mix of locals, tourists, scientists, skeptics, believers, and very dedicated cosplayers
Accessibility	Citywide event with outdoor and indoor venues; family and wheelchair friendly
Cultural Significance	One of the most famous conspiracy-related festivals in the world
Fun Fact	You might find a retired Air Force officer discussing radar tech *right next to* someone describing their latest alien abduction over a glowing green snow cone.

McMinnville, Oregon

But Roswell isn't the only town that's turned cosmic curiosity into community celebration. McMinnville, Oregon's UFO Festival[13] sprang from a famous 1950 photograph of what appeared to be a flying saucer hovering over a local farm. Today, the festival combines Pacific Northwest craft beer culture with cosmic contemplation – where else can you sample 'Close Encounters IPA' while debating the authenticity of declassified government documents?

During my visit to McMinnville's festival, I found myself judging an alien pet costume contest alongside a NASA engineer and a local brewing legend. The winning entry? A chihuahua transformed into a convincing Xenomorph, complete with extending inner jaw made from a modified party favor. The festival has become a crucial tourism driver for McMinnville's historic downtown, with businesses reporting their highest revenue during the three-day event.

⚲ McMinnville UFO Festival – Tourist Fact Sheet

Category	Details
Name	McMinnville UFO Festival
Location	McMinnville, Oregon
Type of Event	UFO-Themed Cultural Festival / Science & Speculation with Local Flavor
Origins	Based on a 1950 photo of a "flying saucer" taken near McMinnville
First Held	1999
Timing	Mid-May annually
Signature Experiences	🍺 Local beer releases like "Close Encounters IPA" 👽 Alien cosplay parade 🎤 Speaker panels with scientists, authors, and believers 🎨 Art vendors, alien swag, and food carts galore
Attendance	One of the largest UFO festivals in the U.S. outside Roswell
Vibe	Equal parts credible inquiry and joyful weirdness
Host Location	Hotel Oregon (McMenamins) — home base and primary event venue
Community Blend	Local families, UFOlogists, sci-fi fans, beer nerds, and the simply curious
Accessibility	Central downtown location; walkable and family-friendly
Fun Fact	Only at this festival can you **debate UFO disclosure** while sipping a craft IPA named after interstellar contact.

Pine Bush, New York

Pine Bush, New York, has taken a more educational approach with their UFO Fair[14], incorporating STEM activities alongside the expected array of cosmic entertainment. I watched elementary school students launch model rockets while their parents attended lectures on astrobiology, proving that even the most whimsical celebrations can spark scientific curiosity. The town's transformation from a place known for mysterious triangular lights in the sky to a hub of space science education shows how communities can evolve their UFO legacy into something both entertaining and enriching.

▦ Pine Bush UFO Fair – Tourist Fact Sheet

Category	Details
Name	Pine Bush UFO Fair
Location	Pine Bush, New York (Hudson Valley region)
Type of Event	UFO-Themed Street Festival with an Educational Twist
Origins	Rooted in decades of local UFO sightings, especially reports of triangle-shaped lights
Timing	Typically held in **May** each year
Signature Experiences	☝ Alien cosplay & costume contests ✦ Model rocket launches for kids ✎ STEM booths & science exhibits ☞ Lectures on astrobiology, exoplanets, and UFO research ☄ Live music, food vendors, and intergalactic fun
Educational Focus	Partners with schools and scientists to promote curiosity and space science
Audience Blend	Families, school groups, skeptics, true believers, and backyard astronomers
Accessibility	Walkable small-town setup, family- and wheelchair-friendly
Community Evolution	From hotspot of unexplained sightings to a **hub for science education & space enthusiasm**
Fun Fact	It's one of the only UFO festivals where you can attend a **lecture on astrobiology** in the morning and **enter a costume contest** in the afternoon.

Tips for Attendees

For those planning to attend any of these cosmic celebrations, here's some earthly advice:

- **Book accommodations well in advance** – hotels in festival towns fill up faster than you can say 'beam me up.'

- **Look for early-bird ticket packages** – many festivals offer access to special events and VIP alien encounters.

- **Bring cash** – some vendors still haven't upgraded their payment systems to accept intergalactic currency (or even credit cards).

Most importantly, pack your sense of humor along with your camera. Whether you're a true believer or a skeptic, these festivals aren't really about proving or disproving extraterrestrial existence – they're about communities coming together to celebrate their unique identity and history, even if that history includes mysterious lights in the sky and controversial government explanations.

The best festivities balance entertainment with education, offering everything from serious scientific discussions to costume contests where dogs dressed as aliens compete for prizes. They're places where retired military personnel can share stories with wide-eyed believers, where amateur astronomers set up telescopes next to face-painting stations, and where the question 'Do you believe?' is always answered with a knowing smile rather than a definitive yes or no.

These celebrations remind us that sometimes the most valuable part of searching for extraterrestrial life is finding human connections right here on Earth. Whether you're sharing conspiracy theories over alien-themed cocktails or learning about space exploration from actual rocket scientists, these festivals offer something far more tangible than proof of alien existence – they offer community, creativity, and the chance to embrace the endless possibilities that exist when we look beyond our earthly boundaries.

Celebrating Quirk: The Soul of Small-Town America

After crisscrossing America in search of its strangest celebrations, I've come to understand that these festivals aren't just about quirky entertainment – they're windows into the soul of small-town America. From garlic-scented streets to alien-themed parades, each celebration tells a story of community resilience, economic innovation, and the peculiar magic that happens when people come together to embrace their local legends, no matter how unusual.

These festivals do more than generate tourism dollars (though they certainly do that, with events like the Roswell UFO Festival drawing over 100,000 visitors annually). They preserve local history, create intergenerational connections, and prove that sometimes the best way to build community is to celebrate what makes your town different – whether that's a weather-predicting groundhog, an abundance of stinky alliums, or a disputed UFO sighting from 1947.

What strikes me most isn't just the creativity behind these events – though watching engineers launch fruitcakes with medieval siege weapons certainly showcases human ingenuity – but the way these celebrations transform potential economic liabilities into cultural assets. Towns with declining industries have reinvented themselves through festivals. Communities facing population loss have found ways to bring their diaspora home each year. Even the most skeptical locals eventually don their tinfoil hats or don their garlic-themed costumes, because these festivals remind us that sometimes the best response to life's absurdities is to organize a parade around them.

Tips for Festival-Goers

For those inspired to explore America's festival circuit, remember:

- **Stay local** – skip the chain hotels and stay at local B&Bs where owners share festival history over breakfast.

- **Volunteer** – working booths is a great way to meet locals.

- **Try the food** – yes, even the Spam ice cream.

- **Join the fun** – participate in costume contests, no matter how silly you feel.

These festivals thrive on participation, not observation.

Most importantly, approach each celebration with respect for its origins and significance to the local community. While many of these events embrace their quirky nature, they're also points of genuine pride for year-round residents who invest countless hours in their success. The celebrations might seem silly on the surface, but they're serious business for the communities that depend on them.

As we wrap up our tour of America's strangest festivals, I'm reminded of something a local organizer told me at the International Cherry Pit Spitting Championship: **"It's not really about how far you can spit a cherry pit. It's about giving people a reason to come home."** In an age of increasing disconnection, these wild and wonderful celebrations provide exactly that – a reason to come together, to laugh at ourselves, and to remember that sometimes the strangest traditions make the strongest communities.

Chapter 11

Conclusion

Reflections from the Road: Embracing America's Weirdest Attractions

As I sit here sorting through a shoebox full of ticket stubs, pamphlets, and slightly questionable souvenir keychains from America's strangest tourist attractions, I can't help but smile at the beautiful absurdity of it all. From the towering roadside giants of the Midwest to the underground bunkers of the Cold War, from UFO-themed motels in the desert to festivals celebrating everything from Spam to space aliens, this journey through America's weirdest tourist traps has taught me more than just the location of the world's largest ball of twine (though that's definitely worth knowing).

What started as a quest to document the bizarre and unusual corners of American tourism became something far more meaningful. In each oversized attraction and oddball museum, I discovered communities of passionate people dedicated to preserving and celebrating the quirky side of our cultural heritage. These aren't just tourist traps – they're living testimonies to American creativity, eccentricity, and the enduring spirit of roadside wonder.

The true magic of these places isn't in their size, strangeness, or even their gift shops (though I've developed quite the collection of questionable postcards). It's in the stories they tell and the people who keep them alive.

- The retired physics teacher who converted his mobility scooter into a Mars Rover at the Roswell UFO Festival.

- The elderly tai chi practitioners finding zen beneath an abandoned roller coaster.

- The proud curator of the International Banana Museum, ready to share his potassium-powered passion with anyone willing to listen.

What I've learned is that the best travel experiences often come from embracing the unexpected, taking that random exit off the highway, or following that hand-painted sign promising **'WORLD'S ONLY'** something-or-other. Sometimes the GPS will try to lead you straight into a smoking crack in the earth (looking at you, Centralia), and sometimes that's exactly where you need to go to find the best stories.

These offbeat attractions remind us that travel isn't just about reaching a destination – it's about the wonderfully weird journey along the way. They prove that America's greatness lies not just in its natural wonders or historic landmarks, but in its capacity to dream up and build the absolutely ridiculous, then convince people to drive hundreds of miles to see it.

So the next time you're planning a trip, consider taking the road less traveled – preferably one that leads to a giant concrete prairie dog or a museum dedicated to sock monkeys. Pack your sense of humor, leave your cynicism at home, and remember that sometimes the best memories come from the places that make you ask, **'Why does this exist?'** Because in the end, the answer is usually, **'Why not?'**

And if you find yourself standing before a massive frying pan in Long Beach, Washington, wondering if you've made some wrong turns in life, remember: you're exactly where you're supposed to be. Just watch out for those low-hanging cave ceilings, keep your passport to the peculiar handy, and never, ever turn down the chance to wear a banana spacesuit – even if the zipper looks suspicious.

After all, in a world of increasingly standardized tourist experiences, these weird, wonderful, and sometimes inexplicable attractions remind us that there's still plenty of magic to be found in the unusual, the unexpected, and the unabashedly strange. They're proof that the great American road trip isn't dead – it's just gotten a lot weirder. And personally, I wouldn't have it any other way.

Safe travels, fellow adventurers.

May your roads be strange, your destinations bizarre, and your stories worth telling.

And remember, if you ever find yourself lost on the way to the world's largest whatever-it-is, sometimes the best thing to do is embrace the detour.

After all, that's where the real adventures begin.

Please Consider Leaving a Review

H ELLO THERE!

As an author, I know just how important reviews are for getting the word out about my work. When readers leave a review on Amazon, it helps others discover my book and decide whether it's right for them.

Plus, it gives me valuable feedback on what readers enjoyed and what they didn't.

So if you've read my book and enjoyed it (or even if you didn't!), I would really appreciate it if you took a moment to leave a review on Amazon. It doesn't have to be long or complicated - just a few words about what you thought of the book would be incredibly helpful.

Thank you so much for your support!

Les

Also by

Our catalog is constantly growing!

Visit AdultingHardBooks.com

For our other titles and free bonuses!

1. Thacker, M. (2024, November 14). *The World's Largest Ball of Paint*. Anderson Madison County Visitors Bureau. https://visitandersonmadisoncounty.com/blog-the-worlds-largest-ball-of-paint/

2. *World's largest pistachio*. (n.d.). https://pistachioland.com/worlds-largest-pistachio/

3. *Oregon Vortex*. (n.d.). Oregon Vortex. https://www.oregonvortex.com/

4. Devil's Rope and Texas Route 66 Museum. (n.d.). *Devil's Rope and Texas Route 66 Museum | Texas Time Travel*. Texas Time Travel. https://texastimetravel.com/directory/devils-rope-and-texas-route-66-museum/

5. *World's largest ball of twine - Cawker City KS, 67430*. (n.d.). https://www.travelks.com/listing/worlds-largest-ball-of-twine/2344/

6. Enchanted Highway. (2024, May 11). *Home - Enchanted Highway*. https://enchantedhighwaynd.com/

7. Gassmann, G. M. (n.d.). *World's largest Catsup bottle official web site and fan club*. http://www.catsupbottle.com/

8. Lucy The Elephant. (2023, July 7). *Lucy the Elephant - The world's greatest elephant*. Lucy the Elephant. https://lucytheelephant.org/

9. Wikipedia contributors. (2025, June 5). *Federal Aid Road Act of 1916*. Wikipedia. https://en.wikipedia.org/wiki/Federal_Aid_Road_Act_of_1916

10. *Oakley, KS - Prairie Dog Town (Closed)*. (n.d.). RoadsideAmerica.com. https://www.roadsideamerica.com/tip/498#google_vignette

11. Tripadvisor. (n.d.). *The Coffee Pot (2025) - All You Need to Know BEFORE You Go (with Reviews)*. https://www.tripadvisor.com/Attraction_Review-g52178-d4819244-Reviews-The_Coffee_Pot-Bedford_Pennsylvania.html

12. Imbler, S. (2019, November 13). The Strange Second Life of Ohio's 'Big Basket' Building. *Atlas Obscura*. https://www.atlasobscura.com/articles/longaberger-basket-building-hotel

13. *The Big Duck*. (n.d.). https://suffolkcountyny.gov/Departments/Parks/Historic-S ites/The-Big-Duck

14. *The Orginial World's Largest "Free Standing" Hockey Stick*. (n.d.) . https://www.evelethmn.com/index.asp?SEC=31CE7DA6-A289-4F7C-B1A6-3 A1FAE1DC915&Type=B_BASIC

15. *Salem Sue: World's largest Holstein Cow, New Salem, North Dakota*. (n.d.). Roads ideAmerica.com. https://www.roadsideamerica.com/story/2716

16. *World's largest Buffalo Monument | Discover Jamestown*. (n.d.). Discover Jamestown. https://discoverjamestownnd.com/fun-things-to-do-in-jamestown-n d/all-things-buffalo/worlds-largest-buffalo-monument/

17. https://www.worldrecordacademy.org/2022/06/worlds-largest-muskie-sculpture -world-record-set-in-hayward-wisconsin-422210

18. *World's largest six pack and king of beer, La Crosse, Wisconsin*. (n.d.). RoadsideA merica.com. https://www.roadsideamerica.com/story/12028

19. *The Mystery Spot official website*. (n.d.). The Mystery Spot Official Website. https: //www.mysteryspot.com/

20. *Oregon Vortex*. (n.d.-b). Oregon Vortex. https://www.oregonvortex.com/

21. *Confusion Hill*. (n.d.). Confusion Hill. https://www.confusionhill.com/

22. *Cosmos Mystery Area – Cosmos Mystery Area*. (n.d.). https://cosmosmysteryarea.c om/

23. *Gravity Hill - Defy Gravity - Bedford County, PA*. (2024, February 13). Gravity Hill. https://gravityhill.com/

24. *Mammoth Cave National Park (U.S. National Park Service)*. (n.d.). https://www .nps.gov/maca/index.htm

25. Joy. (2025, March 10). *Bunker Tours - the Greenbrier Resort*. The Greenbrier Resort. https://www.greenbrier.com/activities/bunker-tours/

26. *Carlsbad Caverns National Park (U.S. National Park Service)*. (n.d.). https://www.nps.gov/cave/index.htm

27. Luray Caverns. (2023, December 31). *Luray Caverns - What will you discover?* https://luraycaverns.com/

28. *Wind Cave National Park (U.S. National Park Service)*. (n.d.). https://www.nps.gov/wica/index.htm

29. *Minuteman Missile National Historic Site (U.S. National Park Service)*. (n.d.). https://www.nps.gov/mimi/index.htm

30. *Oscar-Zero Minuteman Missile Alert Facility (U.S. National Park Service)*. (n.d.). https://www.nps.gov/places/oscar-zero.htm

31. *Jewel Cave National Monument (U.S. National Park Service)*. (n.d.). https://www.nps.gov/jeca/index.htm

32. Wikipedia contributors. (2024, December 2). *Nevada State Route 375*. Wikipedia. https://en.wikipedia.org/wiki/Nevada_State_Route_375

33. *E.T. fresh jerky*. (n.d.). E.T. Fresh Jerky. https://etfreshjerky.com/

34. *Little A'Le'Inn – Earthlings welcome*. (n.d.). https://littlealeinn.com/

35. https://travelnevada.com/extraterrestrial/black-mailbox/

36. BlueSoft. (2025, June 6). *Exciting Day Tours from Laughlin | Desert Wonder Tours*. Desert Wonder Adventures. https://desertwondertours.com/

37. *Www.virginiawright-frierson.com*. (n.d.). https://www.virginiawright-frierson.com/The-Bottle-Chapel-at-Airlie-Gardens.php

38. *Ave Maria Grotto*. (n.d.). AVE MARIA GROTTO. https://www.avemariagrotto.com/

39. *Salvation Mountain - Official Website - Niland, California*. (n.d.). https://www.salvationmountain.us/

40. *Wisconsin Concrete Park | Travel Wisconsin*. (n.d.). TravelWisconsin. https://www.travelwisconsin.com/museums-history/wisconsin-concrete-park-203838

41. *Dickeyville Grotto*. (n.d.). Dickeyvillegrotto. https://www.dickeyvillegrotto.com/

42. *Ave Maria Grotto*. (n.d.-b). AVE MARIA GROTTO. https://www.avemariagrotto.com/

43. *Rudolph Grotto Gardens*. (n.d.). https://www.rudolphgrotto.org/

44. *The official Watts Towers Arts Center campus*. (n.d.). Wattstowers. https://www.wattstowers.org/

45. *House on the Rock - Wisconsin Attraction | Resort | Golf*. (2025, May 12). House on the Rock. https://www.thehouseontherock.com/

46. Bishop Castle. (2025, May 7). *Bishop Castle - Adventure to New Heights | Official website*. https://www.bishopcastle.org/

47. *Howard Finster's Paradise Garden | Chattooga County, GA*. (n.d.). https://www.chattoogacounty.gov/186/Howard-Finsters-Paradise-Garden

48. *African Village in America, Birmingham, Alabama*. (n.d.). RoadsideAmerica.com. https://www.roadsideamerica.com/story/24361

49. Mercer County Convention and Visitors Bureau. (2022, August 31). *Lake Shawnee Abandoned Amusement Park - Mercer County WV*. Mercer County WV. https://visitmercercounty.com/places/lake-shawnee/

50. Wikipedia contributors. (2024a, October 2). *Rocky Point Amusement Park*. Wikipedia. https://en.wikipedia.org/wiki/Rocky_Point_Amusement_Park

51. Ugc. (2025, June 10). Heritage USA. *Atlas Obscura*. https://www.atlasobscura.com/places/heritage-usa-2

52. Encyclopedia of Arkansas. (2023). Dogpatch USA. *Encyclopedia of Arkansas*. https://encyclopediaofarkansas.net/entries/dogpatch-usa-2302/

53. Rachel. (2021, July 9). *Exploring abandoned Chippewa Lake Park*. Third Stop on the Right. https://www.thirdstoptontheright.com/chippewa-lake-park/

54. Cowan, E. (2022, April 25). *Joyland Amusement Park*. Abandoned Kansas. https://abandonedks.com/joyland-amusement-park/

55. Legend City in metro Phoenix: Look back in time at the beloved theme park. (2024, April 29). *The Arizona Republic*. https://www.azcentral.com/picture-gallery/entertainment/life/2024/04/29/legend-city-phoenix-photos/73445639007/

56. Hedding, J. (2019, June 6). *CrackerJax Family Fun and Sports Park*. TripSavvy. https://www.tripsavvy.com/crackerjax-family-fun-and-sports-park-2681851

57. Wikipedia contributors. (2025a, February 18). *Compton Terrace*. Wikipedia. https://en.wikipedia.org/wiki/Compton_Terrace

58. Tripadvisor. (n.d.-a). *Devil's Rope and Route 66 Museum (2025) - All You Need to Know BEFORE You Go (with Reviews)*. https://www.tripadvisor.com/Attraction_Review-g56261-d270412-Reviews-Devil_s_Rope_and_Route_66_Museum-McLean_Texas.html

59. Penka, B. (n.d.). *Kansas Barbed Wire Museum*. https://www.rushcounty.org/BarbedWireMuseum/

60. Towing Museum. (n.d.). *Towing Museum*. https://towingmuseum.com/?gad_source=1&gad_campaignid=22475158557&gbraid=0AAAAA-6WXeck4b5Cl7WIHZ9-q3JfYCn4g&gclid=CjwKCAjwr5_CBhBlEiwAzfwYuAkH19kmYbqVyIrc9ZRVdENQ78Kx7O4FETC3EBBec8s9fBKRnqgzxRoC_dMQAvD_BwE

61. *museumofquackery.com: Bob McCoy: founder of the The Museum of Questionable Medical Devices*. (n.d.). https://www.museumofquackery.com/

62. *Toaster Museum Foundation, Charlottesvil VA*. (n.d.). https://museumsdatabase.com/museums/view/33085

63. Quest Digital - A Digital Marketing Company. (n.d.). *Pencil Sharpener Museum*. https://www.explorehockinghills.com/things-to-do/arts-museums/museums/pencil-sharpener-museum/

64. The Umbrella Cover Museum. (n.d.). The Umbrella Cover Museum. https://www.umbrellacovermuseum.org/

65. *SPAM® Museum in Minnesota | SPAM® Brand*. (2025, May 30). Spam. https://www.spam.com/museum

66. *National Mustard Museum*. (n.d.). National Mustard Museum. https://mustardmuseum.com/

67. *JELL-O Gallery – Historical LeRoy Jello Gallery*. (n.d.). https://jellogallery.org/

68. *THE INTERNATIONAL VINEGAR MUSEUM*. (n.d.). The International Vinegar Museum - Roslyn, SD. http://www.internationalvinegarmuseum.com/

69. *Idaho Potato Museum*. (n.d.). https://www.idahopotatomuseum.com/

70. *Creation, Science, Bible History, & Dinosaurs*. (n.d.). Creation Museum. https://creationmuseum.org/

71. *International UFO Museum & Research Center*. (n.d.). Roswellufomuseum. https://www.roswellufomuseum.com/

72. Stark's Vacuums. (2023, December 1). *Stark's Vacuum Museum in Portland OR | The History of Vacuums*. Stark's Vacuums - Vacuum Store & Repair Services. https://starks.com/about/vacuum-museum/?srsltid=AfmBOoqiW25qVomxMe084qgPa2EiYfGmOezIFo8ljSpYx0q4ZX8mbBqL

73. *Heart attack grill*. (n.d.). https://heartattackgrill.com/

74. Warerkar, T. (2020, March 5). Ninja, the wacky restaurant once declared a critical disaster, closes after a long 15 years. *Eater NY*. https://ny.eater.com/2020/3/5/21166070/ninja-restaurant-nyc-tribeca-closure-japanese-sushi

75. *The Airplane Restaurant - 1 block East of Powers Boulevard on Fountain Boulevard, Colorado Springs, CO.* (n.d.). The Airplane Restaurant. https://theairplanerestaurant.com/

76. Denny's Beer Barrel Pub. (2021, October 28). *Denny's Beer Barrel Pub - Burgers & More Clearfield PA.* https://dennysbeerbarrelpub.com/

77. Stansky, J. (2025, June 10). *Welcome to the Winchester Mystery House® - Winchester Mystery House.* Winchester Mystery House. https://winchestermysteryhouse.com/

78. *Solomon's Castle.* (n.d.). http://solomonscastle.com/

79. Parks, C. S. (n.d.). *Bodie State Historic Park.* California State Parks. https://www.parks.ca.gov/?page_id=509

80. Wa, D. C. I. S. (2025, May 14). *Home - Visit Pioneer Square - Seattle, WA.* Visit Pioneer Square - Seattle, WA. https://pioneersquare.org/

81. Wikipedia contributors. (2025c, June 7). *Centralia, Pennsylvania.* Wikipedia. https://en.wikipedia.org/wiki/Centralia,_Pennsylvania

82. Bodie.com. (2024, July 31). *Bodie, California | Methodist Church.* Bodie, California. https://www.bodie.com/history/structures/methodist-church/

83. *Bannack State Park | Montana FWP.* (2020, October 22). https://fwp.mt.gov/stateparks/bannack-state-park

84. *Guidotti Castle, agricultural and courtyard appurtenances (Castello Guidotti, pertinenze agricole e cortilive) – Ducato Estense.* (n.d.). https://ducatoestense.com/en/estensi/guidotti-castle-agricultural-and-courtyard-appurtenances-castello-guidotti-pertinenze-agricole-e-cortilive/

85. Ugc. (2025a, June 6). Tom Kelly's Bottle House. *Atlas Obscura.* https://www.atlasobscura.com/places/tom-kellys-bottle-house

86. *BOTTLE VILLAGE.* (n.d.). BOTTLE VILLAGE. https://bottlevillage.weebly.com/

87. *EMMA CRAWFORD COFFIN RACES & FESTIVAL*. (n.d.). EMMA CRAW-FORD COFFIN RACES & FESTIVAL. http://www.emmacrawfordfestival.com/

88. Ugc. (2025b, June 9). International Cherry Pit-Spitting Championship. *Atlas Obscura*. https://www.atlasobscura.com/places/international-cherry-pit-spitting-championship

89. *Frozen Dead Guy Days 2025: A "Freeze"tival of Fun in Estes Park*. (n.d.). https://frozendeadguydays.com/

90. Western Minnesota Steam Threshers Reunion. (2025, February 20). *Western Minnesota Steam Threshers Reunion - Rollag, MN*. Western Minnesota Steam Threshers Reunion |. https://rollag.com/

91. *Gilroy Garlic Festival | July 25–27, 2025 | Garlicky Food & Fun in Gilroy CA*. (n.d.). https://gilroygarlicfestival.com/

92. *Waikiki spam jam*. (n.d.). Waikiki Spam Jam. https://www.spamjamhawaii.com/

93. *Midwest Tomato Fest - Minneapolis, MN*. (n.d.). Yelp. https://www.yelp.com/biz/midwest-tomato-fest-minneapolis

94. Manitou Springs. (2025, May 5). *The Great Fruitcake Toss - Manitou Springs, Colorado*. https://manitousprings.org/events/fruitcake-toss/

95. Punxsutawney Groundhog Club. (2025, May 13). *Punxsutawney Groundhog Club - the home of Groundhog Day!* https://www.groundhog.org/

96. *Bee Cave Bob from Bee Cave, Texas*. (n.d.). https://groundhog-day.com/groundhogs/bee-cave-bob

97. *Pierre C. Shadeaux - New Iberia, Louisiana*. (n.d.). Pierre C. Shadeaux. https://countdowntogroundhogday.com/groundhogs-around-the-world/Pierre-C-Shadeaux

98. *General Beauregard Lee from Jackson, Georgia*. (n.d.). https://groundhog-day.com/groundhogs/general-beauregard-lee

99. McMenamins UFO Fest. (2025, May 19). *McMenamins UFO Festival*. McMenamins UFO Festival. https://ufofest.com/

100. *UFO fair | The Pine Bush UFO & Paranormal Museum*. (n.d.). The Pine Bush UFO & Paranormal Museum. https://pinebushmuseum.com/ufo-fair

www.ingramcontent.com/pod-product-compliance
Lightning Source LLC
Chambersburg PA
CBHW052115030426
42335CB00025B/2995